How To Be A Bad Muslim

And Other Essays

Mohamed Hassan

16pt

Copyright Page from the Original Book

PENGUIN

UK | USA | Canada | Ireland | Australia
India | New Zealand | South Africa | China

Penguin is an imprint of the Penguin Random House group of companies, whose addresses can be found at global.penguinrandomhouse.com

First published by Penguin Random House New Zealand, 2022

1 3 5 7 9 10 8 6 4 2

Text © Mohamed Hassan, 2022

The moral right of the author has been asserted.

All rights reserved. Without limiting the rights under copyright reserved above, no part of this publication may be reproduced, stored in or introduced into a retrieval system, or transmitted, in any form or by any means (electronic, mechanical, photocopying, recording or otherwise), without the prior written permission of both the copyright owner and the above publisher of this book.

Design by Carla Sy © Penguin Random House New Zealand
Cover photograph by Joel Moriasi
Prepress by Soar Communications Group

A catalogue record for this book is available from the National Library of New Zealand.

penguin.co.nz

TABLE OF CONTENTS

1: Subscribe to PewDiePie	1
2: The witch of El Agouza	19
3: Showdown in the Kōwhai Room	35
4: The last sober driver	42
5: The day I tried to live	53
6: My country, my country	67
7: A stranger in no man's land	82
8: Ithaka and the lonely god	93
9: Always watching	100
10: Ode to Elliot Alderson	115
11: How to be a Bad Muslim	124
12: The curse of the Bosphorus Strait	154
13: Therapy with Ivanka	169
14: The peace of wild things	189
15: Still life with a pool of dreams	203
16: A pirate's life	207
17: A letter unsent	222
18: Two funerals	229
19: 10 stages of Arabic love	240
Acknowledgements	249
About the author	250
Back Cover Material	253

i

for Zayn and Zak

Self-radicalisation

in a cold neon room
the men with sharp eyes
tell me I need to be

more open
more concubine

I want to stretch out my eyes
blue as anything holy
so they will look over me

I want to rip off my white collar
and show them
and the rest of the audience
how ugly my ancestry looks
in a circus tent

1

Subscribe to PewDiePie

IF YOU WERE HEAVILY ON YOUTUBE at any point over the past ten years, then you would have had run-ins with the Swedish streamer Felix Kjellberg.

Through an unholy mix of circumstance, a cunning eye for relevance and an untethered penchant for shamelessness, Kjellberg had become an entity that eclipsed the video platform. One of the first to adopt gaming online as a way of attracting an audience, he quickly amassed a following drawn to his knowledge and ability, but especially his off-colour commentary on both the games and his virtual rivals.

Pretty soon he was filming, editing and publishing videos daily, expanding his archive to include meme reviews, reaction videos, and reaction-to-reaction videos. As YouTube grew into a community of recognisable content creators with their own loyal audiences, whose galaxies inevitably collided with one another, there emerged a need for social commentators who could poke fun at the ridiculousness of two strangers arguing from their bedrooms. Kjellberg became a kind of online jester, egging on his peers, sharing cringe posts and taking shots at the tech giant that hosted them.

It might not need explaining if you have seen any of his content, but the thirty-two-year-old man who screams 'PewDiePie' at the top of each video and turns his voice into a nasal high pitch to mock feminists mostly attracts an audience of teenage boys. They idolise him, dedicating subreddits to memes, fan art and referential jokes about his episodes, hoping he'll pick out one of them to showcase in his weekly fan service. His theme song and intro animations were made by fans, and his engagement with his audience incentivises them to keep interacting, and to stay loyal. He's also not afraid of the criticisms he faces for how young his audience is, often referring to them as his 'nine-year-old army' in self-referential jabs. They of course embrace it as well, buying t-shirts and other merchandising with the label printed proudly in obnoxiously loud type. It is the internet after all, and everything can be repurposed for the sake of humour.

And it's here where PewDiePie creates the most chaos. Many times in the past ten years his face has been plastered across blogs and mainstream news sites for provocative jokes made knowingly or in the heat of a two-hour Twitch livestream.

In one incident, he called another player the n-word for killing him in a *Call of Duty* game. In another he almost said it, but backed away and made a joke about how he's not going to give his critics fuel to attack him. In another incident, he donned a Nazi uniform and sat down in front of a TV screen playing a speech by Hitler, apparently to highlight the dangers of taking his videos out of context. The result was that the clip was taken out of context and reported on by *The Wall Street Journal* and other outlets.

Each time he got in trouble, his pubescent army rallied to his defence. Other YouTubers did as well, accusing the media of conspiring against the content creator. On Reddit he became a martyr, said to be unfairly targeted by mainstream liberals who were out of touch with youth and the internet. In return, media commentators painted Kjellberg as one of the figureheads of the emerging alt-right movement, which had stepped out from the shadows in the era of Trump. Critics suggested that Kjellberg, like other cultural provocateurs who made their name on the internet, was deliberately messaging to an audience of men's rights activists, disgruntled White middle-class gamers and self-described 'edgelords' railing against the progressive liberal politics of the world around them.

It became self-fulfilling: the more negative attention he and his fans attracted, the more they dug in their heels.

In 2017 Kjellberg pulled a stunt that backfired on his own career in real ways. While scrolling through the website Fiverr, where you can pay five dollars to request services and products from a database of freelancers and giggers online, he decided to test just how far someone would go to earn the fee.

A week later, he unveiled his achievement: a video of two young Indian men holding up a sign that said 'Death to all Jews'.

The fallout led to YouTube pulling the original series it had produced for Kjellberg months before it was to air on its subscriber platform Red. Another content platform, Maker Studios, owned by Disney, also dropped his sponsorship. Jewish groups around the world denounced him. He even made it to cable news programmes. PewDiePie couldn't shrug this one off.

The man who revelled in mocking other YouTuber apology videos found himself in front of the camera doing just that. He backed away from the stunt, saying it was just an example of his brand of 'absurd' humour that shouldn't be taken seriously. Once again, his fans saw their hero admonished in the public light.

None of this had an impact on his independent reach and financial success. His apology video was watched by 7 million people. He began to release two videos a day instead of one, and to host more frequent livestreams that netted him hundreds of thousands of dollars each month in advertising revenue. By this point, he had amassed a subscriber base of close to 60 million. If he was a king, his country would be larger than South Africa.

But this was only the beginning, because in 2018 fate handed him a golden chalice that would make him more powerful than anyone could have predicted.

The chalice was called T-Series.

T-Series was an inconspicuous channel on YouTube that published Bollywood music videos, operated by a large production company who wanted another avenue to promote its films and rising stars. There wasn't much to it, really—it was just one of thousands of other music-related spaces where Bollywood lovers could congregate to watch and share their favourite songs lip-synced by their favourite actors, obviously with the industry's impeccable choreography and costumes.

But in 2018, India was joining the digital world, thanks to the wonders of high-speed internet. Within a few short years, infrastructural developments had connected around 20 per cent of the country, and for the first time, more than 200 million people were able to access Facebook, Twitter and of course YouTube. Seemingly overnight, thousands of new channels started popping up to cater to this new audience. Thousands more content creators and YouTubers were setting up makeshift studios from their bedrooms and reacting to the latest Indian news and entertainment. Most importantly, people could now watch their favourite Bollywood clips online and on demand—and there was a lot of demand.

Within a few months, T-Series ballooned, drawing in first thousands, then millions, then tens of millions of viewers and subscribers. This threatened the once untouchable dominion of our friend and the people's hero, PewDiePie.

Internet commentators placed bets on how long it would take before Kjellberg's channel was overtaken. Others set up websites where the subscriber numbers of both channels could be watched live. For the first time since the birth of the internet, a non-English, non-Western platform was about to rule, and that made some people very uncomfortable.

Many creators were upset that a corporate-run channel without original content was dominating their space, and railed against the precedent it would set for the future of their beloved platform. Others turned their noses up at the 'cringe' songs and dances and wondered why anyone would find them entertaining. Subreddits exploded with angry jokes at the expense of the channel and its owners, encouraging them to take their 'inferior' culture elsewhere.

In the midst of this hurricane of teenage angst and new media puritanism, an unlikely messiah emerged to carry forth the torch of authenticity. Like Daenerys Targaryen slowly hoisted by the unshackled hands of the Yunkai, the rightful king of YouTube heard the call of his destiny. PewDiePie would save us all from the darkness beyond the wall.

It began organically—a simple call by fans rallying their community to take action against this external threat. A collective action that was simple, easy and straightforward:

#SubscribeToPewDiePie

If the hordes of foreign users were propelling an unworthy content channel to the top of the subscriber table, then the loyal tastemakers of YouTube would make sure they never got there. All it took was a simple click, and you could cast your vote for Felix and his cultural vanguard of nine-year-olds. The campaign dominated the platform for months, drawing support from other influential content creators like Logan Paul,

MrBeast and Casey Neistat. They all encouraged their fans to support Kjellberg in what became a defence of the internet as a space for free and equal individual expression, and a rejection of corporatisation in the interest of profit. For a while it appeared to be working, with millions of people uniting to push the PewDiePie channel further and further ahead of the encroaching T-Series. At first, Kjellberg laughed off the rivalry, poking fun at the impact and reach of his fanbase. But soon, he realised his audience was beginning to skyrocket and his video views were increasing, and that meant more exposure and money than even he had been able to achieve before.

After the campaign slogan had ricocheted around the halls of the internet, Kjellberg began to embrace it himself. He recorded a parody rap diss track titled 'Bitch Lasagna' to declare he was officially challenging the music channel. The lyrics were intentionally cringy, but at its heart were the 'nine-year-olds of worlds' taking on the large population of India, who were told to 'hold your defecation'. It was no 'Mamma Mia'.

By the end of 2018, he had grown his channel from 58 million subscribers to 90 million. It was a feat never before achieved on YouTube, and only surpassed by the likes of world-leading athletes like Ronaldo and Messi on Facebook and globe-topping celebrities like Beyoncé and Ariana Grande on Instagram.

The diss track has had close to 300 million views on YouTube, and has been streamed 100 million times on Spotify. It wasn't well received in India, where Kjellberg was sued by the owners of T-Series for what they described as racist and vulgar attacks on their brand. Kjellberg eventually settled the lawsuit with the company, but the video remained blocked in India following a decision by the Delhi High Court.

Inevitably, the T-Series channel overtook PewDiePie, exploding past its humble beginnings online. By 2021, it had 200 million subscribers, with an incredible 160 billion views on its videos. Another Indian-based channel, SET India, emerged and quickly grew to 120 billion, while the American nursery rhyme channel Cocomelon had 122 million desperate parents.

For Kjellberg's efforts, he was rewarded with another 20 million subs—placing him fourth in line with an audience of 110 million—and conceded defeat to his rival by releasing another parody track titled 'Congratulations'. The song was far from conciliatory, explaining that it took 'a billion Asians' to beat a single Swedish boy, and that India should 'figure out how to fix the caste system' before getting on YouTube.

That song was also blocked in India.

In the 2017 book *Kill All Normies*, Angela Nagle chronicled the turn in online culture from the naive optimism of the late 2000s—when everyone was listening to Kanye's backpack anthems, voting Barack Obama into office through the viral 'Yes We Can' campaign and scheming to overthrow Joseph Kony through clicktivism—to a descent into cynicism the following decade. As online forums like Reddit, 4chan and 9GAG began to build a shared language around pop culture memes and complex, ever-evolving inside jokes, acronyms and references, a new dogma began to form. This online world would reject the sincerity of Tumblr and early-stage Facebook, and cleave to a darker doctrine, one steeped in the harsh realities of a world haunted by economic recession and climate catastrophe. There was no room for authenticity. All emotional expression had to be conveyed through self-deprecating humour, and presented without motive. Nothing was out of bounds, nothing precious or sacred was safe from ridicule, and to be included in the zeitgeist, you had to have the stomach to joke about dead babies and the Holocaust. If you got offended, you just didn't get it.

Hidden in the forgiving shade of this circus tent of impertinence were those with more complex intentions. As Nagle documents, crawling under the skin of the forum community were a group of people who could conveniently mask their real hatred and misogyny in edgy memes. They made racist and sexist jokes and no one batted an eye, because no one really meant what they said. Not on the internet.

Over time, a motley crew of angry young men began to take the reins of the forums, whipping their peers into a frenzy whenever they were challenged. During the so-called Gamergate saga, their targets were female game journalists documenting the lack of representation in video games. These journalists found themselves hunted by thousands of anonymous accounts, who sent death and rape threats to their emails, hacked into their IP addresses and published their addresses and phone numbers online. The internet suddenly became a place where an unpopular opinion could make you a target. Some wannabe cultural leaders rode this new wave to their own successes, the most prominent being Milo Yiannopoulos, who went on to become one of the founders of the alt-right movement. Others like Kjellberg tapped into the anger of young gamers worried their favourite platforms would get ruined by heavy-handed political correctness that insisted on centring female characters and dampening the steroid-injected violence they loved to escape into.

Those maimed by the unrelenting acidity of this battle retreated to safety, and those who embraced the chaos emerged as the new leaders of the internet.

Meanwhile, social media platforms like YouTube, desperate to capitalise on their exponential growth of content, rushed to build algorithms that not only accommodated it, but encouraged their users to consume it at incredible rates. Recommended lists of videos now appeared on the right-hand sides of browsers based on what the code predicted each user would find interesting, or irresistible, based on what they'd engaged with. The more extreme, the higher the likelihood the user would click out of curiosity, and the longer they'd remain within the confines of the platform. Soon the video-sharing platform that brought us classics like 'Charlie Bit My Finger' and 'lonelygirl15' was now a haven for far-right conspiracy prophets warning against mass immigration and feminism. These videos were watched by millions and shared on other online forums where their merits were discussed, creating a feedback loop that repeated the same ideas louder and louder until they drowned out reason. Conspiracy theories about White genocide and Clinton-funded paedophile rings operating out of pizza shops bounced around the internet, collecting disciples and reaching alarming heights.

A month after the US presidential election in 2016, a man entered the Comet Ping Pong pizza restaurant in Washington DC with an assault rifle and began firing, convinced he was rescuing children from sex slavery. It was the first sign that the once seemingly harmless meme politics of the internet had left the keyboards and entered the Real World.

Eight months later, hundreds of White supremacists marched through Charlottesville, Virginia, carrying torches and Nazi flags and shouting 'Jews will not replace us'. It was a coalition of angry men who had spent years stewing in the cesspits of the internet, who helped elect a far-right president who seemed to believe the same conspiracies as they did, and who promised to reshape the world in their image.

Halfway across the world, a young Australian man was watching this unfold with keen interest. He devoured their messages and felt them resonating in his own disjointed life. He spent hours engaging in online communities and seeking out those who saw the world the way he did, who felt outcast and oppressed by the politics in their societies, and who had decided they needed to take things into their own hands.

When forums like Reddit and 4chan began clamping down on the extreme segments of their user bases, they migrated to offshoots like 8chan that accommodated their ideas. Here they were free to speak openly, shedding their masks of irony and embracing their shared grievances.

Here, Brenton Tarrant felt right at home.

For months, he meticulously pulled together a plan he hoped would immortalise him among his peers. He fantasised about his name echoing across history, evoking pride in the hearts of young men looking for a hero to take up their cause. The world around him seethed with destruction and evil, and he would not stand by while his culture and his people were written out of schoolbooks and picked apart by those less worthy. White men like him were in danger, and he would not sit idle and watch a demographic genocide unfold before his eyes.

He wrote down his thoughts in an extensive document, outlining his master plan, his justifications for it, and the revolution he predicted would be triggered by his actions. Once he was done, he gave it a title referencing the vast conspiracy playing out in Western cities all over the world, fuelled by greedy, business-minded corporate elites and their rich Jewish friends with sinister intentions: 'The Great Replacement'. The phrase had been spreading across the internet for years, born from the mind of the ageing French writer Renaud Camus, who titled a 2011 book *Le Grand Remplacement*, hoping it would shake European society awake to the demographic tsunami engulfing them.

'The great replacement is very simple,' Camus told *The New Yorker*. 'You have one people, and in the space of a generation you have a different people.'

The phrase was championed by Canadian alt-right darlings Lauren Southern and Stefan Molyneux, who arrived in New Zealand in August 2018 to warn Pākehā they were letting in too many immigrants, and too many Muslims in particular. When a public uproar pushed a local council to cancel their venue bookings, their fans were enraged. They accused the government of shutting down free speech and public debate, of giving in to the whims of leftists and 'genocidal Marxists', to borrow a phrase from Jordan Peterson.

Tarrant, too, must have seethed at the news. He knew that his plan was needed more than ever before, to shake the sleepy masses around him into action. The strange and foreign cultures worming their way into civilised cities, built off the sacrifices of his grandparents and their grandparents, were unscrewing the bolts of enlightenment. White people would soon be outnumbered in their own homes, and then it would all be over. He had to act, and soon.

The morning he chose was awash with opportunity. He closed his eyes and smiled, rolled down the window of his car and let the late summer air caress his clean-shaven chin. The route off the motorway and into the heart of Hagley Park was imprinted on his corneas. He'd made the drive between Al Noor Mosque and Linwood Islamic Centre dozens of times, timing it on his phone, counting the traffic stops, the Friday-morning traffic, the time it took for two small mosques to fill to capacity.

He kept his sunglasses on while he eyed a police car driving past. Kept his cool. The guns were all in the trunk and out of sight, alongside his military-grade bulletproof vest, helmet and GoPro camera. He resisted the urge to check the 8chan forums, where he'd just uploaded his manifesto, but imagined hundreds of people sifting through it keenly over their morning coffees, sharing it with their friends, dreaming of a better tomorrow. He also sent a copy to his family, alongside a cryptic farewell. It wouldn't matter—they would find out soon enough.

Through the wrought-iron fencing he could see the worshippers greeting each other at the doors of Al Noor Mosque, taking their shoes off and making their way into the dimly lit corridor that opened up at the end into a large congregation space where hundreds sat cross-legged on a freshly vacuumed carpet. Most were still dressed in high-vis vests and sweaty button-up shirts from the morning shift at work. Others in pristine white-and-cream thobes and shalwar kameez. Opposite them sat Imam Gamal Fouda, his eyes closed, going over the finer points of the sermon he was about to give.

A few minutes later, when quiet had resumed on the narrow street, and only the wild mating calls of the cicada and the faint laughing of children could be heard, Tarrant slowly turned his car into the driveway and shut off the engine. He opened the door and walked calmly to the boot, where his holy arsenal laid out, awaiting him. He donned his protective gear over his camouflage overalls, and strapped a large hunting knife to the pocket of his vest alongside seven automatic rifle rounds. He attached the camera to the front of the helmet, lifted it over his head, and clicked the straps into place. He squeezed a handgun into his holster, and lifted up his AR-15 semi-automatic rifle. For a second he admired his work, the white markings he had made all over the barrel and handle in correction fluid. The martyrs of his revolution would all be here with him, and soon he would be with them.

His livestream had already begun, and as he gently let the lid of the trunk fall, he thought about the 400 people who were rapt in his performance, and felt pride expand in his lungs. For months, he'd spent restless nights in bed imagining this single moment, what it would feel like, and what he would say to commence his orchestral masterpiece. One breath. Two. He lifted the rifle to his chest and pointed it at the entrance. The show was about to begin.

He only had one message left to impart to the audience watching at home before he walked inside. It was perfect, really. They would understand.

'Remember, lads, subscribe to PewDiePie.'

2

The witch of El Agouza

WALKING INTO ANY ARAB HOUSEHOLD, THERE are a few things you're likely to experience.

The first is the unmistakable scent of incense, the smoky musk of oud floating in the indoor climate, clearing out all that has persisted before it. In Egypt it's tradition to light the bukhoor before guests arrive. Kind of like a red carpet rolled out, masking the smell of onion, garlic and cumin that had ruled the house for hours while the matriarch carefully prepared a feast that could feed dozens. In a similar vein, if they can afford it most Arab households have two living rooms in their homes. Some families sacrifice a dining room in favour of that second, more prestigious *salon.*

Once when I was twelve and visiting Cairo to celebrate my aunt's engagement, I caught her and her dashing fiancé kissing in the salon after they'd been left alone by the rest of the household. I freaked out, thinking I had intruded on something unseemly, and reacted by throwing myself on the floor and crawling to the opposite side of the dining room like a foot soldier behind enemy lines, or Tom Cruise in between running scenes. After I grabbed my Walkman from my bag and returned to the safety of the hallway, making sure I used the dining table as cover, I heard them both sniggering. They were probably watching me the entire time.

It's also tradition to light bukhoor on Fridays, the holiest day of the week for Muslims, when they wash, don their finest clothes and their most impressive cologne, and head to the mosque for the weekly Jumaa prayer. Because it's a holiday in most of the Muslim world, the men usually return from prayer to an early lunch and the mesmerising scent of oud. Then everyone takes a nap. Afternoon naps are a sign of true living. In Greece and Spain, people swear siestas are the secret to long life. In the Arab world, where life expectancy is still only in the late sixties, people use it as an excuse to stay up all night. In Cairo summers you can find restaurants packed with families at four in the morning. By 8am they'd all be at work and school, chirpy and alive the way Egyptians always seem to be. I never understood how anyone got anything done.

In working-class Sufi neighbourhoods, bukhoor is also used to ward off evil spirits, devils and jinns. It's part of a deep culture of superstition continued through generational practice. Another is hanging up passages from the Quran on your front door or from your car's rear-view mirror to protect yourself from jealousy and the evil eye. During Eid ul-Adha (the festival of the sacrifice), when Islamic tradition encourages people to slaughter a cow or sheep and disperse the meat among those less fortunate, some leave handprints of cattle blood on the backs of their recently bought microbuses or pickup trucks. You can tell that a driver's recently come into some money or a new vehicle if they have bloody handprints on their rear bumper.

But my favourite of these rituals is the one I grew up watching my grandmother perform every Friday. I would come back from prayers in the early-afternoon heat and sit and watch her pull out an old newspaper from a basket in the corner of the living room where she had collected them since the 1990s. She'd sit in her favourite armchair and carefully unfurl the paper over the coffee table. Sliding her thick reading glasses down to the tip of her nose, my grandmother would meticulously cut out human figurines from the centre of the paper. She'd collect several leaves together so her cutouts would give her a handful of little paper people.

Once she was done, she'd gather up her little family and carry them into the kitchen. I would follow quietly after her and sit on the wooden stool at the mouth of the narrow room, while she headed for the stovetop oven near the window.

After turning on the gas and sparking a fire over the burner, she picks up the first little paper person with her left hand and holds it above the fire with her right hand. Her reading glasses microscope in on what was once an article about a children's book fair opened by Hosni Mubarak's wife, Suzanne. Now the article, and the reporter trapped in its byline, are also embroiled in this sacred ritual.

As the heat licks the feet of the cutout, my grandma produces a needle out of thin air and feeds it into the heart of the little paper person. It rips clean through, leaving a tiny hole that quickly becomes a portal smoke whispers through. She brings her arm back gently, then stabs swiftly forward into the spleen. Then back out and through the centre of the mouth.

The silent figure twists and wriggles in the heat, the holes in its body glowing amber white as its legs catch fire and curl up. Soon she lets go. I watch transfixed as the upper torso takes flight, disintegrating into thin air, leaving a hot flash of light and a puff of smoke.

Before the ashes of the sacrificed find rest on the corner of the stovetop eye, another is brought forward, a needle emerges, the ritual continues.

Grandma's tongue clicks softly as she recites a passage from the Quran, or a secret prayer, or the names of everyone she loves. I could never pick up the words, and it seemed too sacred a space to interrupt with immature questions. So I would sit in silence, and watch.

There must've been a week when she missed this, because one Friday when I was eight years old, the witch arrived.

She appears first in my sleep, when I am defenceless and under the influence of preteen anxiety, trying to decipher the world around me. I wake up in the middle of the night, busting to go to the bathroom. I crawl out of bed and stumble bumble-eyed into the corridor stretching from the living room to the big bathroom. For some reason, I don't turn towards the toilet. Instead, something is drawing me the other way, to the mouth of darkness that has swallowed the salon. I am the only one who's awake, or so I tell myself. When I reach my grandmother's armchair and the basket of old newspapers, something moves in the corner of my eye. My neck snaps left, but nothing. I take two more steps into the dark, wait for something to move again. It does. I turn my head to the dining room and see a shadow of a snake gliding through the air. The snake dances and weaves, before transforming into a pair of long black gloves emerging from the wall. Against my own wits, I move a step closer to investigate, and my curiosity is rewarded. My aunt Aliyah emerges from behind the fridge, laughing with childish glee.

In her late twenties, she had decided to don the full niqab for a few years. It consisted of a long black veil that covered most of her body, a face veil tied to flow over her nose and mouth and drape down her chin, and long black nylon gloves that stretched to just below her elbows. It's not a requirement in Islam for women to wear the niqab, though cultural traditions in the Gulf, rural Syria and Afghanistan have maintained it for generations. In other countries, like Egypt, the practice became popular in the late 1990s during the rise of political Islam. By 2007 more than 90 per cent of Egyptian women wore the hijab, but only a fraction of them were drawn to the niqab. It was a stark contrast to previous decades, when veiled women were looked down on as uneducated and poor. My aunt would later go back to wearing the classic hijab, but not before she and I made a tradition of playing this game in the living room, where she'd turn her black gloves into puppets and dance them up and down from behind the wall, dismembered from the rest of her grinning body.

Now, standing in my dream in the shadow of the living-room curtains thrown by the corridor's neon bulbs, I let down my guard and move closer to embrace my aunt, who's still laughing at having tricked me.

But I don't make it to her before dust lifts suddenly off the floor tiles and begins to swirl around my feet. The window panes rattle. The corridor bulbs flicker. Slowly, as if on cue, I turn my head towards the front door of the flat. I know something is coming. I watch the gentle light creeping through the bottom of the door frame darken as a figure approaches from the space beyond. Soon it's covered completely, and the gold-plated door handle shivers, then twists suddenly down.

The door is flung open, hurling orange light into the living room and a wild wind with it. There, standing with shoulders hunched and legs wide apart, is the witch.

Whenever I try to remember her face, I inadvertently picture the Wicked Witch of the West from *The Wizard of Oz*, which I didn't watch until I was twelve years old. She wasn't from the 1990 film *The Witches*, which I saw much later. Perhaps she was from the Disney classics I watched as a child, notably *Snow White*. The Evil Queen was a chilling figure, even before her transformation into the old woman brandishing off-market apples. Whatever version of evil had cemented itself into the back of my childhood subconscious, here it stood before me.

I had the witch dream over and over when I was eight years old, and it always ended the same way: with the witch breaking open the front door of my grandmother's flat and standing in the doorway, her figure drenched in black, her body silhouetted against the dusty orange glow from beyond. A portal to hell or the unknown. I could always see her face, tilted down, eyes leering out from beneath her crooked black hat. A deep and knowing grin squirming its way up the sides of her cheeks.

This witch terrifies me. Her presence sends chills rolling through my bones. I stand in the centre of the living room, transfixed, unable to move or speak. Slowly the witch raises her arms towards me. I feel my feet begin to lift from the ground, the dust around them swirling faster and faster. When I am floating inches above the ground, the witch draws her hands towards her chest—pulling an invisible rope, pulling me in. My body obeys, drifting slowly towards the doorway and further away from my aunt and the life I know.

I try to scream for help to my aunt, who's still twirling her black gloves from behind the kitchen wall, unaware of the calamity befalling me, but there is no sound coming out of my mouth. I scream and scream, but nothing.

My body moves faster and faster through the air towards the witch, whose high-pitched cackles seep into my bones until it feels as if her voice alone is reeling me in. Her jagged fingernails clasp at the air between us; she pulls and pulls and pulls. I look back one last time at the living room I grew up in, the family I love, the world I know so well, and prepare myself for the abyss.

Then I look the witch in the eyes, which are burning now with an otherworldly flame. They widen, welcoming me into her dimension. Her arms extend. The orange light bellows.

I wake up.

This dream always took place in my grandmother's house. While my mother was working at the state broadcaster, an iconic building resting on the Nile referred to as 'The Television', I would spend my days hanging out with my grandma and my aunties, and later my baby cousins, until it was time to go home. This was my whole world. But when I turned eight, I suddenly found I was being pulled away from it.

I don't quite remember when I was told that we were moving abroad. I remember watching milk ads on TV in my bedroom. They showed rolling green hills and pristine white sheep, and ended with a mysterious name: New Zealand. What planet was this? It certainly looked nothing like the concrete jungle I could see from the balcony of our ninth-storey apartment. There were no people in these ads, just vacant-eyed sheep eating from an endless expanse of grass. Was this heaven? Was it hell? I didn't know.

All I knew was it was strange, and I didn't like it.

My dad had gone ahead six months before us to look for work, and set up a base for us to follow him. My mother was as nervous as I was, leaving everything she'd ever known to fly to the edge of the world with three kids in tow, braving immigration officers speaking a language she could barely navigate in. My brother and sister were too young to really register what was happening, but for me, eight years old, it felt like the world was ending. I would be leaving my family, my friends, my school and my bedroom with posters of Kevin Sorbo's *Hercules* for the complete wilderness beyond my imagination. (I would learn years later that my favourite childhood show was actually filmed in New Zealand, and later again that Sorbo wasn't as cool as I had imagined.) It was all happening against my will and without any consultation.

And so, in the absence of control, my mind tried to make sense of the situation in my sleep. It was a way to unjumble the universe that was expanding beyond my control. Life as I knew it was being pulled into an abyss. The idea of diaspora was a shrouded witch like the ones I watched through my fingers in movies.

I've always had an overactive imagination. This would help me conjure up worlds I could lose myself in, both great and, later, terrible. Cocoons spun from wonder and shadows, protecting me when the universe expanded too fast or began caving in, betraying me when I lost sight of the stars. Often when we examine our childhoods, we can trace our narrative arc to the place where our hidden truths emerged, to the time the magic we believed in became entrenched, as we aged and shed our outer skins. My mum later told me that I had always been an escape artist, but that instead of running away physically as many kids do, I would retreat into these other dimensions. Sometimes for hours. Other times for years.

I must have had the dream about the witch a dozen times. It's the only recurring dream I can remember having. Each time was just as vivid; each time I'd wake from it scared and confused, the way children do. The way adults do.

When we finally did move to New Zealand, on 15 May 1997, a new chapter of my life began. The experience would be confronting, but would ultimately teach me to expand instead of contract. To find my voice as a poet and the bravery to celebrate it out loud. To be an artist in a garden that nourished me in a way the melancholia of an ageing civilisation could not.

The scale of the sacrifice my parents made is difficult to understand. Their worlds were shattering too, and their transition to a new one would be tumultuous and scary. The world they were thrown into did not offer them the same leniency it afforded me. But together, we pushed out, ready to face the unknown.

These days, almost every Egyptian dreams of diaspora, of escape. When I speak to my cousins in Egypt, I can hear the tiny hints of jealousy. They live in a crumbling city. A country that demands loyalty to its golden past, but offers nothing in return for its future. The Arabic name for Cairo translates to 'the conqueror', but it is a stark irony. It has always existed to be coveted by the greatest empires—the Greeks, the Romans, the Ottomans, the French, the British. Anyone with weapons and ambition has tried to take it at one time or another. Its people, rough diamonds carved under thousands of years of pressure, laugh with their eyes and dream in the ashes.

When I speak to my grandmother on the phone now, I try not to ask her about how the country is doing. She is full of sadness. The buoyant 1960s she knew, when men wore Italian suits and women smoked long black cigarettes that matched their silk miniskirts, is a distant memory. She watches now the bones of her city creaking. The air thick with failed industry and paranoia. The decorated revolutionaries that overthrew the foreign kings and promised a new world now perched on the chests of her grandchildren. Nobody dreams there anymore. They have been taught not to.

She lives alone in the apartment by the Nile where she has spent most of her life, where she was once young and in love with a man who planted kindness in people's eyes. Now he sits watching from a framed painting in the living room, looking over her favourite chair where she sits to play Facebook games on her laptop, or fill out the weekly crossword in a newspaper she'll later throw in a straw basket until the next witching hour.

I was born in a hospital down the road from this house. The name of the suburb is immortalised on my passport (causing confusion at every airport I visit): El Agouza. In Arabic it has a peculiar meaning—'the old woman'. It's not clear who this woman is, or why the municipality was named in her honour. Perhaps she was the wife of a Turkish pasha who remained long after the Ottoman Empire collapsed. Perhaps it is a metaphor for the city, an ageing matriarch who danced wildly and sensually through her youth, and now rests in her favourite chair, caressing her aching legs and the memories held in them. Or perhaps the name belongs to an old witch, who cursed the city and stole its children.

When I ask my grandma about her sacred newspaper ritual, she laughs in surprise. It has been a while since she's done it.

'I learnt it from my mother, of course. God rest her soul.'

Before moving to Cairo in her teens, my grandmother was raised in the heart of Upper Egypt, where ancient magics and local superstitions are held sacred. Watching an episode of the Hulu show *Ramy*, I clapped with joy when one of the characters, suffering from sudden hair loss, visits an Egyptian witch in New Jersey, who makes cutouts from newspaper and burns them above a fire to undo a curse that caused it. My grandmother explains that the ritual wards off the effects of the evil eye, a concept firmly believed by Muslims to govern their world, as real as gravity or taxes.

'Our religion tells us to be wary of people who can cast the evil eye on us. When someone suddenly falls ill, or a newborn baby is overly complimented by strangers, we have to watch out for that.'

In the Quran, there are passages that Muslims are instructed to read if there's a suspicion that an evil gaze is afoot. We're taught to say *ma shaa Allah* when complimenting others on their good fortune. It simply means 'what God wills', and is intended both to guard the person from evil and ourselves from jealousy. We're taught to say *in shaa Allah*, 'if God wills it', when we make plans, in case something gets in the way and stops them, or some evil plots against us.

My grandmother tells me we can cast the evil eye on those around us without realising, which is why we have to be careful, and read the Quran as often as possible. We also have to be thankful for things we are blessed with, like good health and offspring, before they are taken away.

She tells me that my phone call has made her day, that she spent the morning bored and lonely, waiting for a distraction. Perhaps it is the curse of old age, to watch those you love leave, one after another, whisked away to other worlds.

What kind of ancient magic or prayer could return loved ones lost to time and circumstance?

She ends our call as she always does, praying that I find the right girl who will make me happy, and that I come back to Cairo, to El Agouza, to live by her side again.

I say, 'In shaa Allah, Teta.'

3

Showdown in the Kōwhai Room

I PUSHED AN EIGHT-YEAR-OLD BOY INTO a rubbish bin two weeks after migrating to New Zealand.

In my defence, it was self-defence. Also, I was eight years old as well, so it was a fair fight. It's hard to tell this story in detail because the child in question is now a celebrated Kiwi sports figure who represented the country on the world stage and reached great heights in his chosen field.

But at the tender age of eight, he was kind of a dick.

We had arrived on a long-haul flight through Singapore with no in-flight entertainment, save for a single screen at the front of our aisle showing a butterfly documentary on a loop for ten hours. I don't know how my mother managed to transport me, my five-year-old brother Sherif and my one-year-old sister Basma between two worlds, but we all arrived at Auckland Airport alive and unscathed. At passport control, an immigration officer smiled down at me, crumpled in a knitted sweater and baby fat, trying to hide from this strange world.

'Hello there.'

I watched a dust bunny bouncing underneath the desk, feeling the heat of the terminal rising.

'Say hello,' my mother nudged.

'Umm ... hello.'

So much for my being top of my class in English. When the officer continued speaking, barely moving his jaw between sentences, I tilted my head and tried to decipher. Surely this wasn't English.

Baba met us at the terminal with a blow-up balloon and new glasses. We were escorted into the back of a sleek Honda Integra. It was the fanciest car any of us had ever ridden in, save for the Chevrolet my grandfather used to own in the 1960s, though I'd only ever heard stories about it.

'Whose car is this?' Mum asked.

'Someone lent it to me,' Dad replied.

'People lend you their cars here?'

'You did, remember?'

Mama blushed. This was my dad's way of telling her this new car he had bought was now in fact hers, and that he was merely borrowing it.

We drove up the nape of State Highway 1, and I craned my neck out the window to marvel at the rolling hills of green hugging the white terraced houses. The buildings were so low, and all that lay behind them was endless sky. As we sped past the city and through Freemans Bay, I looked out and saw water in every direction. The sun ping-ponged off the surface and lit up the underside of the Harbour Bridge, stretching its back out over to new land beyond. I looked at my brother, the crystal blues in his eyes a storm of delight, and I smiled. This wasn't a scary chapter in our lives after all, this was something new and wonderful.

Our house sat conveniently at the centre of Nile Road, and we were surrounded by caterpillars, new migrants and kind, old faces. In the morning, I packed my valiant green backpack and marched to the gates of Milford Primary School, which fought for its claim on the waters of Lake Pupuke with wildly aggressive ducks. In the icy spring mornings, we would pair up and carry little kayaks down the side of the hill and into the seaweed at the edge of the lake, trying to sidestep through the minefield of seagull and duck poo some of our peers fell victim to.

In my primary school in Cairo, I had sprinted through the curriculum, earning a certificate for the highest marks in my grade. Now I sat at the back of class staring blankly at a teacher speaking in tongues. On the weekends my cousins Dalia and Nada would teach me phrases they had mastered in their three years of expat life.

'Who cares!' they sang in unison as they danced around their living room.

'What does that mean?'

'It means you're a cool guy.'

I also began to learn that for some reason I was no longer the same as the other kids. When I stuttered through my ESOL-grade English trying to ask for a red crayon, I got weird stares in return. Eventually I gave up and sought out other kids with weird accents and better food. The one thing immigrant mothers never understand is that feeding your child well makes them a target. I arrived at school with a lunchbox filled to the brim with feta sandwiches one day, koshari another day, and the sweet smell of basbousa. Big mistake.

'Eww, what is that?'

'Mohamed smells weird.'

I spent a few lunchtimes eating in the empty classroom alone, willing time to move faster until I could be reunited with my brother and sister and we could resume our latest adventure. School began to make me feel anxious, a new world whose rules I never quite understood. Kids wouldn't always be nice to you just because you were nice to them, and trying to be invisible only made you stick out more.

One afternoon, as I was unbuckling the clips on my lunchbox, two of my classmates entered the room. One was very tall, even at that age. His name was Gareth and we'd later become friends. The other was shorter but confident, an athletic kid at the top of the Year 4 social pyramid.

Their eyes looked mean, full of intention. I stood up and held my lunch to my chest, preparing for a showdown.

'What do you have there?'

'Food,' I replied, after thinking about it for a while.

The short one said something snarky—I didn't understand it, but could tell from his tone it wasn't nice—and started pacing towards me with his chest out. I looked over at Gareth, who watched uncertainly but made his presence known. His looming figure stepped between me and the classroom door, while his shorter friend stepped forward, cornering me between two desks near the window.

Then the first push came, knocking the lunchbox from my hands and on to the floor. A Glad Wrapped sandwich hit the ground, feta granules falling out of a rip in its side. A banana bounced a little further, smacking the foot of a chair and finding rest out of sight underneath the arts and crafts table.

'Whay are yoo doing a ziss?'

It's hard sounding tough in a thick Egyptian accent. The response was another shove, knocking me back a few feet. Freed from cradling my lunch, I decided to retaliate, bringing my arms up in a defensive stance Mayweather would have appreciated, and stepped forward. The hardened gleam in his eyes disappeared, and he found himself in motion, his arms flying up above his torso while his feet fought for balance.

Gareth's eyes widened. He looked over at his superior, who had landed inside a large plastic rubbish bin, his bum wedged deep in its mouth and his legs flailing on either side. The next time I saw him, he was standing on a field before the world, a silver fern stitched across his jersey, his hand over his heart as 'God Defend New Zealand' echoed from the stands. He would still look exactly the same, his boyish features and bright eyes fleshed out and fuller, but it was him, alright. We would all be proud of him then, representing our wee country against all expectations. But that wouldn't happen for another two decades. On a sunny afternoon in May 1997, he was stuck in a primary school bin while a weird foreign kid stood above him, tears in his eyes, a broken feta sandwich gasping for life in his hands. It was an image right out of an '80s coming-of-age story, the bullies with their scrambled bravado, the new kid in school transformed from weirdo to hero, championed by his peers and upsetting the playground hierarchy.

Except no one saw it. We'd been in an empty classroom, and now I was in the corner crying and piecing my wounded sandwich back together. I walked out into the sunlight with *Clair de Lune* playing somewhere offscreen, having learnt a lesson about new beginnings, or the appropriate way to wrap lunch for maximum durability. Across the playground sat a fuzzy-haired boy eating koshari from a two-minute-noodle cup. He was the other Egyptian in the school, Pierre. We'd hang out a bunch of times before he'd try to convert me to Christianity during morning tea, and we'd later become adversaries on the football pitch. But not today. I walked over quietly and sat down next to him and we shrugged off our English and mused about the fall of man or our favourite Power Rangers.

Mine was the blue one.

4

The last sober driver

I HAVE NEVER DRUNK ALCOHOL, BUT I have thought about it. I often wonder what it would taste like, what place it would take me to. Would it elevate me into gleeful lightness, or trap me in the depths of my own darkness?

Once, my best friend in high school lashed out angrily at my repeated refusal to engage.

'You think this makes you a man 'cause you don't drink? It doesn't.'

I didn't take his bait, but weeks later, in a school assembly about the dangers of binge drinking and peer pressure, I felt a hot indignance swelling inside me, and hoped my friend was listening and feeling ashamed.

It wasn't a difficult choice for me. It was simply outside the realm of my allowances as a Muslim—back when the world was a thin straight line and good and bad were binaries. Now I'm older and adulthood is a flat weave of complexities. I have more Muslim friends who drink than those who don't. It is not something I judge them for, though I can tell they feel judged by my mere presence. To walk into a party as a sober Muslim is to turn on the lights suddenly at a rave. You feel like someone's dad showing up to drag his son out by the collar to an uncertain fate. My own dad practised discipline through silence, like a monk who refuses to answer your questions about the meaning of the universe, until one day you are screaming in desperation at an unrelenting sun and suddenly you come upon your truth.

In the same way, I too use silence as a weapon, even if I don't intend to.

Whenever I enter a space where alcohol is present, everyone gets uncomfortable. First comes surprise: 'Why not?' Then it turns into confusion: 'You never drink? How do you have fun?' Next it becomes interrogational: 'So you've never even had a sip of beer?' Finally, comes bargaining: 'Just try it, bro, I won't tell anyone.'

If you've ever been to a Muslim wedding, you know we don't need alcohol to cause a riot. I have sweated through three-piece suits dancing for hours with Arab uncles re-living their youth, holding two breadknives between their fingers and swinging their hips to the beat. The heat from a hundred bodies soaking into the ageing wooden beams of a community hall that will air itself out in time for Sunday school the next morning. I've danced until the bride's family was gone and I was left packing up the chairs. We're crazy enough without the liquid courage. We turn up at the drop of a hat.

Remember the Arab Spring? Completely sober.

The anti-Islam film riots that paralysed Sydney in 2012? Sober.

That video by rapper M.I.A. with the Saudi teens driving Range Rovers on two wheels while screaming with their heads out the window in the face of all logic and reason? Yup. Sober.

But at a house party in Mount Eden surrounded by bodies swimming in their own stomachs and telling you they're having a great time—I get nervous and quiet. I don't belong here.

Growing up in a country that loves its drink was difficult. Every social interaction seemed hinged on alcohol, from high-school parties to office functions to networking events to open mics. Everyone I met felt guarded until alcohol opened them up. Workplace friendships were formed at Friday-night drinks. Romantic pursuits seemed only conceivable when both parties were loose enough to be vulnerable. Evening television slots were a cocktail of jovial Tui beer ads about enjoying the summer with the boys, followed by grim drink-driving ads touting the now famous slogan: It's not the drinking, it's how we're drinking. Was it really not the drinking?

Christmas parties were the worst. It's almost an unspoken social contract that it's the one day each year where no limits are abided. No one needed to be at work the next day. Everyone was drunk enough to not pay attention.

Everyone except this guy.

I would remember every messy thing that happened, every racist thing that was said, each awkward romantic gesture left unrequited on the office floor. I was the silent witness to all of it, and as a result no one trusted me.

My friend Carrie Rudzinski wrote about the experience of being the only sober person at a party in her poem 'Carburetors'. At least, that's how I've always read it. It's one of my favourite poems.

> There is no leaving now: only the nausea
> of coming and going,
> a breeding ground of answers that don't
> stand for anything.

In the innocent summer of 2012, Kendrick Lamar released his breakout single 'Swimming Pools (Drank)', catapulting him from a prophesied Compton rapper that hip-hop heads were excited about, to a sudden staple at North Shore parties. I once had the misfortune of being stranded in a corner of a stranger's living room after a theatre show, watching a pack of White kids yelling every word to the song's vital hook, making sure to annunciate the n-word in the first line while they raised their Heinekens to the ceiling.

They seemed to miss the irony that the song was actually about alcoholism and peer pressure, but then again, so did every club in the world that year.

I went to see Vince Staples play the Powerstation a few years later, and left reeking of other people's pints and cradling the unshakable memory of watching hundreds of middle-class White men chanting: 'I ain't never ran from nothing but the police.'

After parties and gigs, I would throw my clothes into the wash before my mum could smell them.

I have often wondered if I was missing out on an integral part of culture, if I was keeping myself on the sidelines of acceptance. Maybe this was the reason I often felt like an outsider.

There were advantages, of course. I saved money each weekend, never having to fork out the costs at bars and restaurants. I've also never had a hangover, though my inherited migraines and natural sensitivity to bright lights have given me an insight into what they might feel like. Why would anyone willingly do this to themselves?

In the first Islamic teachings, alcohol wasn't immediately ruled out. Much like modern-day New Zealand, pre-Islamic culture in Arabia saw plenty of drinking. It was one of the few pastimes nomadic tribes had to stave off the harsh realities of desert life—the long unruly summers, the cripplingly cold nights. Early Arab poets wrote odes to alcoholic drinks. Each region had its own brand, made with everything from anise in the Levant to grapes in Turkey.

Ancient Egyptian pharaohs traded in it, indulged in it during rituals and celebrations, and exported it to the rest of the world. It's said that beer was originally invented by the Egyptians, an accidental byproduct of the agricultural revolution circa 10,000BCE.

When the Quran was first revealed to Prophet Muhammad in the Hejaz region of Saudi Arabia, there were no requirements for how to be a Muslim except for belief in a single god. The act of worship itself wasn't outlined until ten years afterwards, when the prophet and those who followed his path were driven out of Mecca and sought refuge in Medina, where he and Islam were embraced. From here, the tenets of what it meant to be a Muslim were slowly outlined.

Once the daily prayers became widely practised, a passage was revealed urging believers not to pray in a state of drunkenness, so that they could comprehend the words they recited. Alcohol was embedded in the culture—it would take a while for followers of the new faith to be weaned off it.

Another passage spelled it out in more direct terms, explaining:
> They ask you about wine and gambling.
> Tell them, there are great harms in them, [even though they bring] some benefit to the
> people, but their harmfulness is greater than
> their benefit.

Later verses would clearly forbid the drinking of all intoxicants, leading to the near-eradication of alcohol across the Muslim world. Of course, cultural practices survived in many of these places. Today you can find long-established bars in Istanbul side by side with ancient mosques. In Iraq, the large Christian communities continued to produce alcohol, and many of the pre-war middle class enjoyed drinking as part of their social fabric. In Egypt, steep import costs on foreign-produced alcoholic drinks prevented their spread through most of society, but cheaper, often illegally made substitutes now fill social events and weddings even in the poorest areas of Cairo.

More religious families and communities still practise total avoidance, and many Muslims consider it a sin to be in the presence of alcohol, even if you don't partake in it yourself. I've dragged my parents to countless poetry events and theatre shows where they sat politely while everyone around them drank, then escaped immediately after the show was over. Inevitably there were times that someone had too much and the mood of the place began to darken. They never complained, but warned me about spending too much time in spaces like these.

It made me feel guilty—knowing they'd come to support me despite feeling uncomfortable in such a foreign environment, clearly outsiders. I often felt this way too, but persisted because I had nowhere I could be myself, where there was a stage and a microphone and people willing to listen. I was transformed there, unbuttoned.

But I still felt like a constant outsider, bartering parts of myself each time I needed to speak. One day I told my friend Viv that I was going to quit poetry. That it had served its purpose but I'd grown tired and needed to move on. I'd signed up for a youth poetry programme, but I would go to the audition the following day and hang up my boots. Put down my pen.

The next day, however, I walked into a room full of young poets from all ages and backgrounds. They spoke truths I grabbed on to. They had an awkward confidence I vibed with. The workshop was run by a group called the South Auckland Poets Collective, made up of social-workers-turned-wordsmiths who specialised in building life rafts for young people like me. Grace Taylor, Jai McDonald and Dietrich Soakai were the first of the group I met, and they ushered me in with open arms. I felt seen and acknowledged for the first time, and this moved a muscle within me that had never experienced the love of motion. The programme was run by young people for young people, without alcohol, filled with words. My plan to quit poetry evaporated. I had arrived at last. I belonged.

In those workshops I found a particular tribe, a group of young men I became especially connected to: Brian, Husam and Rewa. We were drawn together by a love of hip hop and an unspoken cultural overlap. We were Egyptian, Burundian, Syrian and Māori. We understood each other's necessities. We understood exclusion, and we wanted to build something new.

A few months later, we started organising shows in neutral spaces—libraries, cafés, lecture halls, churches—and to our surprise, people from our communities started filling them. Our parents came. Our younger siblings and their friends. Other Muslims and Polynesians and Africans and kids who couldn't legally get into bars, and others who just didn't like being in them. It was eye-opening and beautiful. Something was shifting.

I had only thought about people from my community. I hadn't considered that there were other communities which felt excluded from spaces that served alcohol; other people who felt unwelcome in them because of their age or appearance or religion or temperament. By creating a space without preconditions or assumptions, the way Grace and Jai and Dietrich had done for us, we filled it with our own energy, and people were drawn to it.

At the second show we held, we invited a musician to play too and ordered pizza for everyone. It was a very 'youth group' kinda move, but it meant that people were fed—another cultural tenet we held close to our hearts. If people were fed, their bodies would be at rest and their souls would be open. The poetry was almost an afterthought. It was an offering to the people who filled our space, and in return they offered us their energies. There was a magic to this that is hard to describe, but was always felt. When I invited new people in, they felt it too. It was a sacred exchange, a spiritual network we were building together. People left feeling full, connected, at peace.

This is not a commentary on alcohol—it's about the intentions we invest. The power we have to create our own spaces, and the beauty of inviting people in.

After these shows, all of my energy was spent. Driving away, the car would be packed with mic stands and papers and empty pizza boxes and a box full of cash which would go straight back into paying for the venue, and the chairs, and the lights and the musicians. When I got home, I'd sit in the quiet with the ignition off, push the seat back and close my eyes.

I'd poured out my insides to a room full of strangers, but had returned a vessel filled to the brim.

5
The day I tried to live

WHEN I WAS SEVENTEEN, I SCRAPED together enough money to buy my first guitar. My concerned mother drove me to the Rockshop on our way home from Sunday school, and I picked out the only thing in my price range—a classical guitar with nylon strings—a hundred dollars.

I spent the next two weeks not leaving the room I shared with my younger brother, Sherif, poring over tabs and chords and watching a million YouTube beginner clips. I painstakingly memorised Spanish flamenco tracks note by note, and sprained my hands stretching to hold bar chords. My fingers blistered and healed, only to blister again. When I managed to learn the D, G and C chords, we were in business. My poor parents must have grimaced through the hours of muffled off-key singing and screaming vibrating through the walls of the house. Soon Sherif joined in and we'd try to harmonise on all the songs we heard on the radio.

Our childhood summers were filled with the sounds of Jay-Jay, Mike and Dom introducing the Top 20 hits each morning in between inoffensively edgy shenanigans like biking down Queen Street naked or prank-calling Jennifer Lopez's hotel room at the Crowne Plaza hotel. I had only been exposed to Western taste for nine years and felt like I had a lot to catch up on. Like most Brown kids I gravitated to gangster rap as a teenager, obsessing over Westside Connection, G-Unit and, to my dad's utter horror, Eminem. He patiently sat through car rides while Marshall Mathers waxed lyrical about his anger towards women and his sadistic fantasies. This definitely wasn't the upbringing my parents had migrated to the West to seek, and it must've filled them with regret to see their children drift so far from the safety of Muslim culture. But by this point, the music had awoken something within me. Soon I began to dig deeper and unearth the roots of hip hop, printing out Nas and Pharoahe Monch lyrics and plastering them above my bed alongside my humble imitations. There isn't an immigrant kid who hasn't at some point dreamt of being a rapper, and I was able to impress my classmates. My obsession lasted long enough that I developed a love for the craft of writing and poetry, but not long enough that I started to seriously plan for a career in hip hop. Thank God.

When file-sharing pirate software like Napster and LimeWire coincided with my regular access to a home computer, I wandered into the underground and alternative, spending my nights drifting to sleep with my headphones on, letting the mind-expanding righteous political ire of Immortal Technique float me through history. When my friends and I hung out, I played them my latest tracks and overwhelmed them with trivia about each artist from my hours of online research. Did you know Mos Def was Muslim, and grew up in the same neighbourhood as Spike Lee? How about that Tupac and Biggie used to be friends, and it was the commercial fight between their label heads Suge Knight and P. Diddy that roped them into their fatal East Coast/West Coast beef?

I had little time for rock then, was unfazed by the middleclass anarchy of Blink-182 or the post-youth-group angst of Creed. None of it spoke to me. But when I started hanging out with White kids in high school who had cultured older brothers I found out about the world I had missed. During a physics class no one had any love for, David asked me if I'd heard of Led Zeppelin. That night, I shut off all the lights and let my Sony Walkman spin the disc I'd burnt before bed. From the first few notes of 'Stairway to Heaven' I knew I was in for a ride. The next few weeks I busied myself with catching up, sprinting through the 1970s and trying to see as many landmarks as I could. The Rolling Stones. Pink Floyd. Genesis. The Clash. The Stooges. Why had no one told me about all this?

My most meaningful friendships were almost always formed around music. For instance, my childhood friend Hassan and I would exchange lists of songs for each other to check out, which we rarely got through completely. Black Sabbath, Living Colour, Jimi Hendrix ... We went to our first ever show—Rage Against the Machine—with our other friend Mado, and went home levitating with excitement over seeing the group back together again, telling us the government was lying to us and that George W Bush should be tried for war crimes.

Or my friend Omar—we would drive around for hours while he played me the latest demos his band had recorded, in between gruelling yet satisfying metal and prog-rock dirges from Dream Theater, Alice in Chains and Type O Negative. We spent ten hours waiting at the front section of the Big Day Out in 2011 so we could be the closest people to Maynard Keenan and Danny Carey once Tool finally began their headlining act. The band played mostly in darkness while a ten-square-metre screen projected a selection of their most obscure music videos. It was utterly psychedelic and utterly terrifying.

Ahmed attempted to rope me into the Auckland hardcore punk scene, but I was too clumsy and calm for the mosh pits and arm swings, and kept searching for melody and songs longer than ninety seconds, of which there were few. They were the only sober spaces I could find that played music, and so I always went even though I clearly didn't get it. I left with a love of Bad Brains and Rollins-era Black Flag, though, so it wasn't a total loss.

Later, in Istanbul, me and Nav clicked immediately over our appreciation of late-stage Kanye. Soon I found Mustafa, who like me had spent years in social isolation unable to find other Arab kids who were into The Strokes, Vampire Weekend and other indie bands only White people were into at the time (at least publicly). Me and Faisal found newage rap gold in Vince Staples and Noname, and he always managed to sneak in a surprise find like the Montreal post-rock band Godspeed You! Black Emperor which confused me at first, then held me captive.

In 2012, while studying journalism at Auckland University of Technology, I volunteered at 95bFM and immediately stepped into a universe where all my music education was useless. I became overwhelmed and intimidated at not knowing about Minor Threat and Lee Scratch Perry—and even more so that I had never listened to local artists that weren't Scribe or Bic Runga. I hid my embarrassingly basic tastes from my colleagues, and turned myself into a sponge. When I was asked to cover for Richie Hardcore's flagship weekly show, I spent all night preparing a playlist of the greatest hip-hop tracks from every era, and proudly announced to the audience that the next three hours would be a crash course on the history of the genre.

If you've ever heard Richie's show, it will come as no surprise that my cute little plan crash-landed in a fiery inferno. Half an hour into back-to-back hip-hop classics by Black Sheep, The Sugarhill Gang and Run-DMC, the first complaints started coming in. An hour later, it turned abusive.

Why are you playing this shit on b?

This isn't Mai FM, asshole.

Where the fuck is Richie Hardcore?

When the bFM programme director Pennie got alerted to the barrage of messages coming in, she raced into the studio and begged me to switch up the playlist. I disgruntledly obliged, and after I played a Killing Joke track people seemed to calm down. When they gave me my own drive show a while later, I started getting better at finding interesting new tunes from across the SoundCloud universe by artists no one had ever heard of, and trawling through the music blogs to figure out what was deemed subversive enough to satisfy the indie crowd. I would still sneak in an Outkast or Missy Elliott track here and there, if only to turn up the volume in the studio and dance myself clean. I started going to more shows and broadening my palate, and it was immensely rewarding. It isolated me from the mainstream that most of my friends were still immersed in, but I found comfort in this secret realm I could disappear to, where I could figure out who I was outside of my community.

There were some artists I could never let go of, no matter how basic they were perceived as being. The most important of these was Chris Cornell, the lead singer of Seattle grunge staple Soundgarden and later Audioslave, which emerged from the ashes of Rage Against the Machine. He was the first singer I was bedazzled by. His voice was superhuman, at once a howling graveyard dog who'd mastered the blues scale and the shrieking spirits harmonising beneath its feet. His lyrics were mournful and ethereal, a feral departure from the focus-group pop and champagne-soaked R&B my radio persisted on playing. At the time I was a wildly depressed kid who struggled to make friends and thought too hard about existence. It was a match ordained by the stars.

When I got my first car, I drove around endlessly screaming at the top of my lungs to 'Cochise', determined to hit the high notes Cornell effortlessly nailed. The first song I taught myself to play on guitar was 'Doesn't Remind Me'. I thought it was the most profound song in the world, and I felt it deeply despite not having any real-life experiences to warrant such sorrow.

Chris Cornell became the soundtrack to my surreal reality. He articulated the darkness, the displacement, the absurdity of young adulthood. How fitting it would be to watch the decadent emptiness of society swallowed up by an ever-expanding 'Black Hole Sun'! To say what you meant, no matter how noisy and loud your expressions of love were. To break free from your cage, rusted and abandoned by the world around you. It was all a little corny, sure, but it was perfectly articulated angst, expressed in a way other lost boys could only dream of. And it was heavy and uplifting, a hedonistic revelry with a misplaced heart on its fists. Me and Chris existed in vastly different worlds, but we were both trying to find ourselves.

What he and his peers rebelled against was post-Cold War triumphalism, the megachurch consumerism of unfettered America that sang its own praises to the world. The most affluent generation in the history of mankind had arrived, but their kids were all depressed and lost.

What I rebelled against was the existential panic of the Muslim world after September 11, whose postcolonial victories had made way only for more insidious imperial dominance, and whose insistence on historical navel-gazing had left it too scattered to figure out what it wanted to say to the world. Under this cloud, the artsy diaspora kids like myself struggled to form an identity that didn't betray the demands of immigrant exceptionalism and the mosque. My parents pressured me because they were programmed for survival. They were raised in an Egypt where conservatism and secularism were tools of control by the state, where social shame was the most powerful currency. And here they were, halfway across the world, in an alien society that greeted them with suspicion and impatience, with children who spoke English and listened to Slim Shady. But I too was trying to survive, because I felt like I was slowly being drained of life by competing voices.

Buried inside my awakening subconscious was a concrete sense of displacement, a feeling that I was constantly in the wrong place, surrounded by people who looked through me. I stumbled into an engineering degree after high school and these feelings became inflamed. I started skipping lectures, avoided group work and only showed up enough not to fail. I snuck into Music 101 and picked up philosophy papers over the summer to water my yearning soul, but it wasn't enough: I still had to return to the gloomy engineering department. It was a long wade through the thick sludge of despondency to make it through each semester.

When I now read the poems I was writing during that time, I am startled by how dark the world around me seemed, how endlessly hopeless. The paths that had been laid out in front of me by my family and society felt wrong, the expectations for a life I was supposed to lead felt hollow. Somebody had handed me a uniform that was too tight and it chafed at the armpits. I felt confined by the clashing definitions of Islam, Kiwiness and masculinity I was steeped in, the boundaries of which continued to close in as I got older. I needed to pursue a financially sound career so I could start a family. I needed to channel my anger into sports, cars and casual misogyny so the other kids wouldn't think I was weird. I had to cheer on the Warriors and drink myself numb so I'd be invited back to house parties. None of it fit, and all of it was dragging me feet first into an abyss I desperately fought to escape.

What I can read clearly now as mental illness felt at the time as the natural and inevitable weight of the life I had been given. My nascent urge to express myself through music and writing would eventually save me from the darkness, once I found spaces and people that allowed me to belong on my own terms, but it would take years until I stumbled across them. One was Ken Arkind, a poet I'd admired in YouTube clips when I was starting to take my writing seriously. I met him when he and another one of my favourite American poets, Carrie Rudzinski, arrived to perform at the Auckland Writers Festival in 2013. They were both disarmingly genuine and made spaces for everyone around them, and both were deeply entrenched in pop culture. Carrie and I bonded over *Harry Potter* and *The Walking Dead*, and Ken and I bro'd out over our eclectic musical tastes. When I invited them to do an interview on my drive show on bFM, I asked Ken what song he wanted me to play for him at the end of the interview. He chose Soundgarden's 'Superunknown'. There was no way we wouldn't be friends after that.

Ken was a '90s punk brat through and through, and knew way more obscure facts about music than I did. We spent hours exploring bizarre theories about Red Hot Chili Peppers guitarists and whether Wyclef Jean actually did his best work after the Fugees broke up. For the record, I stand by the fact that *The Carnival* is superior to *The Score*, and I'm willing to die on that hill, Ken.

As I slowly but surely began to swim towards the light, and the storm in my mind began to settle, my music tastes began to brighten. I returned to hip hop and found new and exciting voices that told relevant and hopeful stories, like Brother Ali, Talib Kweli and later, Chance the Rapper. I started learning to play songs by Alabama Shakes and The National and I started to feel more settled. Post-grunge was dead and gangsta rap gave way to a melting pot of new sounds. The internet's universe was expanding, and now everyone could find their subreddit of like-minded weirdos to geek out with.

Chris Cornell's music started to become more hopeful too. He sang about coming out of depression when his daughter was born, remembering friends lost to the pandemic of aimlessness he had escaped. He wasn't making earth-shattering songs anymore, but they still felt necessary and nourishing. His cover of 'Billie Jean' is still the only convincing and inventive interpretation of Michael Jackson I've ever heard, and before you suggest it, no I don't think The Weeknd's anemic nostalgia pop counts. Even in his mid-life, when most of his peers became caricatures of themselves, Cornell's highly elastic voice aged and mellowed. This granted it a growly warmth that made his love songs bittersweet and his reflections poignant. It felt like wisdom, like the weary kindness of former addicts or Muslim converts.

But life is rarely a straight line, and scars have a way of reopening years on. During my last week in New Zealand in 2017—before I'd trek off to Istanbul for a theurgic new stint in my life—I was at dinner with Ken when we got distressing and unexpected news. Chris Cornell was dead.

His end had come following a string of other untimely celebrity deaths: Prince, Philip Seymour Hoffman, David Bowie, Robin Williams. It had been a bitter few years, and the internet eulogised each one through a string of memes and digital tears. We had learnt how to grieve as a collective online, but not yet how to heal. We joked glumly about our mental health, the apocalyptic state of the world, our inability to form lasting relationships, but we didn't talk about how to deal with the heaviness of it all, to see the world in more than muted shades and inevitable loss.

I drove Ken back to his house, then we sat in the car listening to the entire *Superunknown* album. He insists both of us cried, but I've always denied it. I just remember us listening to Chris opening and closing the vast expanse of his lungs and summoning a searing fury that felt like a higher truth. He wasn't the first friend either of us had lost to suicide, and wouldn't be the last. His illness was a part of life we had both grappled with in its ugliest forms, one I had once obsessed over and narrowly abandoned. We listened to every song, each lyric swelling with preminiscence.

When the final reverbed notes of the final song of the album, 'Like Suicide', concluded, we sat in silence and let the heaviness fall where it needed to. We hugged each other, and Ken promised to see me again before my flight. He held on for an extra second, then said: 'I love you, bro.'

It was earnest and carefully placed, as everything Ken says always is. A small and buoyant light fluttered in my throat.

'I love you too.'

6

My country, my country

ISRAEL ADESANYA MAKES VIOLENCE LOOK LIKE poetry. He dances across the octagon with his long arms flailing and a Machiavellian smirk stretched across his face.

He is a witty fighter, juggling his bravado like a jester whose amusement is a front for a deeper, subversive stab at the king. He tucks and weaves around limbs with such nonchalance it doesn't seem like he's taking things seriously. He twists his weight into a sudden hook, jumps back and cartwheels with one hand. He shakes his torso to imitate fear. He laughs.

It must be infuriating to face him, because he also happens to be one of the best mixed martial arts fighters ever to grace the stage. I have never had the stomach for the sport myself, but even I watch his fights, mesmerised by his ability to seem weightless, unconfined.

Known as 'The Last Stylebender', Adesanya is not afraid of attention. His Twitter bio reads: 'follow me from a distance!' and sits under a profile pic of him topless with two middle fingers held up to the camera, reminiscent of Tupac Shakur at the height of his defiance. He makes off-colour jokes and laughs at them, eggs on his critics and refuses to back down. He also can't seem to shirk controversy, once apologising for saying he would make an opponent 'crumble like the Twin Towers'. Another time he thrust his hips into the back of another fighter in a final act of humiliation after defeating him. The provocations are very much a part of his brand.

Just weeks after he was named the Sportsman of the Year at the 2019 Halberg Awards, Adesanya stood in a dressing room in Las Vegas, mentally preparing for a night that would cement his longevity in the sport. Maybe he checked his Twitter, the way some of us impulsively do every few minutes when we're alone. Maybe he saw his name trending and assumed it was fans hyping themselves up before the big fight, chanting his name virtually around the world. Isn't that what every athlete dreams of?

Except that night people were talking about something else. Another New Zealand athlete, ex-cricketer Scott Styris, had a point to make.

'Can't wait to watch Nigerian Israel Adesanya fight tonight #Halbergs.'

Styris, among others, was angry that Adesanya would walk into the arena carrying the flag of Nigeria, his place of birth. The former Black Cap went on to elaborate that someone who clearly wasn't proud of being Kiwi shouldn't be given New Zealand accolades. It was a big talking point online, and even more so on talkback. Radio hosts wondered rhetorically whether it should be a requirement for high-profile athletes to promote New Zealand colours on the world stage. Perhaps the Sportsman of the Year title was better deserved by someone else.

All this over a flag.

It was pointed out by many that Ultimate Fighting Championship rules dictate fighters are announced according to their place of birth, not their nationality, and that Adesanya has fought under the New Zealand flag many times and has the silver fern etched on his fight kit. It didn't stem the outrage. As an immigrant with two homes, he was expected to prove his loyalty.

But Israel Adesanya does not give a fuck what people think.

'People might not like me representing New Zealand, but what are they gonna do about it? Huh? Exactly—nothing.'

II

AS PRIME MINISTER OF NEW ZEALAND, John Key attempted to change the country's flag in 2015. It was part of a legacy he saw for himself, forever remembered by history as the leader who finally did it.

There were a lot of great reasons to change the flag design. First, and most importantly, it's almost indistinguishable from Australia's flag, especially for those who belong to neither country and hence have no stake in the matter. At sports competitions and world summits, commentators continuously mistake the two teams, only adding to the assumption most of the world has that we are actually part of Australia. My friends make this mistake all the time, and they know I'm from New Zealand. It's infuriating.

Secondly, there's already another flag on it: the British one, sitting smugly in the corner judging the rest of the blue cloth and Southern Cross. It's an obvious and unflinching colonial symbol and a constant reminder of the violent roots of the country's settlement. The flag also fails to represent indigenous Māori culture or people, something it also has in common with its twin from next door.

Thirdly, it's kinda boring. Yes, I know it is a sacrilege deserving of capital punishment, or at least deportation, to criticise a flag you swore an oath in front of. But am I wrong? If we were to imagine a piece of fabric that somehow encompassed all that we cherish and believe in, shouldn't it have a little more pizazz?

Those were all important reasons to change our flag. But what happened? The government spent more than twenty million dollars on a design process that involved hundreds of designers, and held a vote on four shortlisted flags chosen by a team of experts (experts in what was a little unclear) plus a fifth later addition. The winner of this referendum, with its black-and-blue block colours and arching white fern, looked more like the logo of a transpacific freight conglomerate than a nation's flag. In fact, many pointed out that it looked suspiciously similar to the Sanitarium logo. An Australian company. Goddammit.

Another vote was then held, only for people to resoundingly vote to keep the old flag in place. Polls showed that many were actually in favour of a change, but disliked the way the process was conducted. Many more felt unrepresented by the final designs. The Laser Kiwi flag, a joke design made in Microsoft Paint featuring a kiwi shooting lasers out of its eyes, became a runaway internet favourite that people still remember fondly today. If only we'd had the guts to unveil that flag to the world with our trademark deadpan wit and revel in the global confusion.

A few years later, after stepping down from office, the now-knighted Sir John told the *Australian Financial Review* that his greatest regret as leader of New Zealand was the failure of the flag referendum. Looking back over his political career, he felt that he should have pushed the new flag design harder, and that could have altered the country's image of itself.

'The reason I wanted to change the flag was to have something that was uniquely New Zealand, so that we could build a more overt sense of national pride.'

III

COUNTRIES TEND TO CHANGE THEIR FLAGS during crucial shifts in their historical narrative, whether through war or revolution or independence. Most countries in the Arab world have near-identical flags because their modern states were created around the same time, overthrowing colonial rulers in the second half of the twentieth century.

The black-white-red combination was picked up for one flag after another, beginning with the 1952 military revolt in Egypt against King Farouk. When soldier-turned-president Gamal Abdel Nasser began championing pan-Arabism and supporting popular uprisings across the region, the black-white-red 'Arab Liberation' flag was seen as the symbol of a new era. It was soon adopted by Syria, Iraq, the United Arab Emirates, Libya, Yemen and Palestine, with some later introducing the Fatimid green into the mix.

But that isn't the whole story. While these four colours have always been used in the region by different dynasties, empires and families, and are present in most of the region's art and architecture, they weren't combined together in a flag until 1916, by a man called Mark Sykes.

If you're wondering why he doesn't have a typical Arab name, it's because he was actually a British colonel and diplomat, who designed the flag to champion Arab revolts against the Ottoman Empire during World War I. It was adopted by Arab nationalists in their fight to shrug off an Islamic empire they had grown tired of, and whose decline presented a glistening opportunity for European powers.

Remember Lawrence of Arabia and his gallant efforts to liberate the subjugated Arab people? In fact, such efforts had more to do with

European diplomats seizing an opportunity to bring down the 'Sick Man of Europe' and divide the resource-rich region among themselves by promising self-determination to its people. This is where Sykes came in, teaming up with his French counterpart François Georges-Picot to draft an agreement that would divide Ottoman lands between the two colonial powers. The negotiations occurred in 1915, just a year after World War I had begun and three years before it ended.

The Sykes–Picot agreement shaped the Middle East in catastrophic ways, creating nation states on imagined boundaries that split ethnic groups in some areas, while forcing rival tribes together in other parts. Most of today's violent conflicts can be traced in part to the nonsensical division of land under this agreement. The Palestinians were stripped of most of their land. The Kurds were divided into four separate nations. The Christians, Shia and Sunnis of Iraq were clumped together (along with some Kurds). Britain decided which of these new states it wanted for itself; France took the rest. You can look at a map of the region today and see the comically straight lines that define each country's borders, as if drawn by a child or, more correctly, a 35-yearold British Orientalist with an overactive imagination but little diplomatic experience.

The freedom the Arabs were promised was only a façade, one they would spend the next half century fighting to tear down. Millions would die fighting for independence from the new colonial rulers, holding flags that were inspired by those same rulers.

IV

WE SANG THE NATIONAL ANTHEM EVERY day before class at Own Heliopolis Primary School. Our tiny white business shirts ironed and tucked in by our mothers, our striped red-and-black ties straightened and pinned to our chests. Across the large concrete plain that constituted both playground and football field, we lined up in two large groups and stood next to our peers before a five-metre flagpole that bore the flag of our nation: the Arab Republic of Egypt.

My country
My country
My country
I pledge my love
and my heart
to you

The red, white and black waved dignified in the heavy morning air. At the heart of the flag rested the eagle of Saladin: the military genius who became the country's vizier and later sultan in the twelfth century CE. Drawn to the ancient Egyptian reverence for birds of prey, which were inscribed on the walls of temples and tombs, he chose to fly the eagle on his own banner as a sign of power and protection. There were other options: the vulture-headed Nekhbet, a winged goddess who protected the kings of Upper Egypt, or the falcon-headed Horus who watched over the Nile Delta. It was believed that all pharaohs descended from Horus's lineage, and thus inherited the power of divinity. Every morning we lined up and saluted these empyrean birds and their children, as our ancestors had always done.

One day when the final school bell rang, we were told we'd have to wait in our classrooms a little longer. The president was travelling from his mansion nearby to an event elsewhere in the city. First, the plain-clothed police would have to file along Salah Salem Street, which stretched fourteen kilometres from Heliopolis through to the edges of Giza, where my grandparents lived. Next, the uniformed officers would cordon off the side streets, the intersections, the bridges. Snipers would be stationed at intervals along the tallest apartment blocks en route, searching for the faintest signs of unrest. Once the stretch of inner city was locked down and secured, a caravan of tinted black limousines would emerge on to the main street and float through the rare silence. On either side, beyond the cordons and stationed policemen, the public sat in their cars and buses and taxis as the procession passed through. Depending on the time of day, the whole ordeal could last between an hour and five, as the traffic slowly clotted in the side streets of neighbouring suburbs.

At the heart of the ordeal was Hosni Mubarak, sitting in the back seat with his signature aviators shielding his face from the world. Every time he was instructed to undergo this strenuous trip, he clenched his knuckles and stared out at the country he owned, the one he needed to be protected from. It took decades of martial law and the might of the police force to keep him safe. He had ruled under these emergency laws since 1981 when he was thrust into the spotlight unexpectedly; the image of his former mentor shot dead in the chair beside him still as fresh as it always had been. In his old age, he refused to let his guard down. Who else would protect this fragile state?

We spent the afternoon making guns out of paper and chasing each other around the classroom. It could have been hours when the convoy finally passed the school. When we heard the car horns outside we all clamoured to the window to watch. Through the dusty glass and beyond the concrete playground and the iron gates, I saw the black cars appear and disappear. Each vessel glimmered in the heat so brightly they looked brand new. At the front of each bonnet, held high by tiny gold rods, two flags waved wildly back at us.

Even as six-year-olds we understood something important was happening. We were in the presence of greatness. As the central car rolled through the street beyond our world, a sheen shot through the tinted glass and caught my eye. As I looked closer, I saw a shadow turn its head towards me, and I swear, for just a tiny second, it was smiling.

V

AFTER THE COLLAPSE OF THE OTTOMAN Empire, Mustafa Kemal Ataturk invented a new story for the Turks. His mythmaking sent a puff of pride through the deflated arteries of a nation whose allies had abandoned it, and whose enemies circled around its carcass, hungry, scheming. Ataturk's image would be cemented into every stone across the country, and the old, defeated flag of the sultanate became the new flag of a republic. He waved it high and defiant, making it into a promise of future glories.

But the new nation had rules. It would shed the religious and cultural ties of the past and vie for European modernity. Traditional clothing was outlawed, religious schools boarded up. Arabic script was slowly stripped away from mosques, schools and textbooks, replaced by a new Latin alphabet. Then later the hijab was outlawed. This Turkey came with a rebrand, and all Turks had to fall in line.

When a fringe military element attempted to overthrow the country's fragile democracy in 2016, thousands flooded on to the streets and faced down the guns with flags. It was a symbol that stretched beyond bitter political and ideological divides.

But the same flag was waved in 2020, as mobs of young Turks patrolled Syrian refugee neighbourhoods in Istanbul and Ankara, tearing down Arabic shop signs and torching cars. Parties waved the flag during election time, vowing to send refugees home and shut down peace talks with the Kurdish minority. The flag here was also a symbol, but one of exclusion and separation. You are not one of us. This flag is not for you.

VI

NARCISSUS STARED IN DISBELIEF AT THE body of water below him. His fingernails were cracked and parched from digging into the dirt at the mouth of the lake, which had begun to erode and slip. He'd been here every day for a month. Or two months. He couldn't remember. It didn't matter.

He only knew he had to return each morning when the sun was high enough to calm the restless blue before him, stretching its surface like a tablecloth and turning it, by the magic of light, into a mirror. Through it, he watched the most beautiful creature smile. Its eyes lit up each time he arrived, looking up with adoration and a hidden flicker of lust. It was a face only angels could have moulded, only a deity could have imagined, staring back at him in mutual wonder. What could this marvellous being teach him about the world, about himself?

The others in his village mocked him for it. They scorned his obsession and called him mad. But that was only envy; they were incapable of witnessing this benediction.

His family noticed one day that he hadn't returned home. They waited until dark settled—nothing. By the following morning they were worried. They searched the town, asking if anyone had seen their boy. The villagers scoffed and told them to go look by the lake at the other end of the forest.

When they approached through the clearing they found his body, face half submerged in water, hands still clutching an image of himself only he could see.

7

A stranger in no man's land

I HAVE ALWAYS BEEN OBSESSED WITH airports. The wide-open terminals. The warm neon glow of duty-free stalls preying on sleepy guilt. The scent of dispensed coffee, industrial floor cleaner and endless possibility.

As a first-generation immigrant, stretched across oceans and time zones, I have spent a lifetime staring up at a flight display board and thinking about my place in the world. As a kid who wore the question of belonging like an ankle monitor everywhere I went, airports were a magical realm where no one belonged. Like me, everyone was a stranger on a journey. Everyone was seeking something they were missing, and this was the in-between place. Not heaven nor hell. Neutral. Safe.

My favourite is Singapore Changi Airport, with its sprawl of stores, waterfalls and indoor cinemas so endless you feel like Keanu Reeves waltzing through a simulation. My least favourite is Denver International Airport—its nauseating '60s pastel décor and inexplicable acid-daze murals of burning forests, children carrying swords draped in the flag and zombie Nazi officers lording over a sea of displaced mothers. Seriously, look them up, and then read the conspiracy theories.

Beyond all my romantic notions, however, airports have a darker underbelly I have become increasingly conscious of. In a time of globalisation and mass travel, airports are also a 'no man's land' where freedom of movement can be upended in the name of national security.

Over the past twenty years, airport security measures have been tight. After September 11, sweeping counterterror laws were passed under urgency to grant customs agents the right to detain and search travellers for hours, unlock their phones and laptops, question them about their travel histories, the contents of their bank accounts, the nature of their personal relationships. Secret lists are made by immigration agencies to highlight high-risk countries—and by extension, ethnicities—and these are mapped over passenger logs to select candidates for special treatment.

Growing up, I watched my hijab-wearing mother pulled aside and swabbed for explosive material every time we transited through Australia. Every time, we were told it was a 'random search' and asked to sign a waiver that offered us the option to comply or be detained.

When I was old enough to travel by myself, I inherited the privilege, watching my name trigger security systems at the passport control desk. Every single time, I fight the urge to reach up to the glass and explain that this happens a lot because of my common name and because of my profile as a military-aged male from a Muslim background who could be radicalised at any moment. Instead I wait quietly while several phone calls are made and my details checked against several other lists. Eventually I'll be allowed a visa after holding up the queue of irritated passengers.

This is the best-case scenario.

In the United States they stamp your passport with 'SSSS'—Secondary Security Screening Selection—and send you to a room in the back with all of the other travellers stuck in limbo at the gates of promise. At LAX once, in 2016, a sympathetic customs officer sighed at the screen and asked me if I always got stopped at airports. A less sympathetic one led me down the hall and smirked as he opened the door and told me to keep my phone shut and my bags outside.

'Welcome to paradise,' he said.

There were maybe fifty of us, mostly Arabs and Asians, alongside one bewildered White guy in the corner. A dozen desks lined the wall, where irritated staff loudly interrogated passengers with basic grasps of English. They asked about their employment history, academic transcripts, relationship status, while reminding them periodically they could be flown back to their home countries at the snap of a finger. One South Korean woman was asked to explain why she had once been suspended from a business course. I was released three hours later, after they called the media company in New Zealand where I worked, to make sure I was in fact employed there. It was humiliating.

A month later, Donald Trump was elected president of the United States, on a platform that included banning Muslims from entering the country. He signed an executive order to that effect in his second week in office, placing a ban on travellers from seven Muslim-majority countries. It unleashed chaos in airports around the country. Thousands were stranded, placed in detention centres or forced to pay for return flights, and missed out on scholarships, employment opportunities and family visits.

In response, protestors occupied the terminals. Lawyers from the American Civil Liberties Union showed up to offer immigration advice to confused travellers trapped inside. Muslims prayed together in front of the airline desks, their allies surrounding them in silent protection. It was an America battling its own demons. My Muslim friends in Denver and Los Angeles told me they were tired of fighting for their dignity.

As a Muslim I was used to being hit with airport security checks, but when I became a journalist I unlocked a new host of challenges. It seemed that while half the world was suspicious of Muslims, the other half felt similarly about reporters. I was now being flagged on two separate lists.

At Tel Aviv airport, they confiscate your passport and send you to a doorless room in the corner of the terminal. There is no fanfare. You're not told what's happening or how long you will wait. You make conversations with the Palestinians huddled around you to pass the time, and eventually an Israeli Defense Forces soldier takes you into a room and asks you to explain your life.

The first time I travelled to Israel, all of my paperwork was sound and I carried two different accreditation letters, one from my news agency and one from the Israeli Press Office. This meant I only waited for an hour and a half, as opposed to the ten hours my friends with Palestinian lineage endured. I was ordered to surrender all my footage to a military office for approval before I left the country, which of course I did not do.

On the way to Egypt once, when I was living in Istanbul, I left my Egyptian passport at home and bought a visitor's visa when I landed in Cairo. I was pulled aside metres from the arrivals door by a police officer who snatched my papers from my hands and flipped through them. He asked me what I was doing in Turkey and, as nonchalantly as I could, I told him I was an English teacher. I'd practised saying it a dozen times under my breath on the plane. In the lobby outside, my family listened to every announcement in case I'd been arrested. When the police later raided a relative's house and locked him up for protesting, they barked questions about which foreigners had stayed with him recently. His parents quietly asked me not to visit for a while.

Six months later, a Palestinian filmmaker we tried to bring to Istanbul disappeared an hour before boarding his flight from Cairo. For weeks neither we, nor his family, knew his whereabouts or if he was alive. He was sent back to Gaza telling of torture and beatings at the hands of Egyptian police officers.

In Tunis, where I arrived to attend a friend's wedding, I absent-mindedly wrote 'media' in the occupation box on the landing form. At the security desk, a sleepy clerk frowned and stared at me, before asking if I was a journalist.

It seemed Tunisia, though it had survived the crushing counter-revolutionary forces that flattened the Arab Spring hopes of its neighbours, still hated journalists. I panicked, and stared back at him for what I am convinced were at least five seconds of dead air before meekly responding, 'No.' His eyes moved back to the form, then he shrugged and stamped my passport.

In 2016 I began hearing stories from friends and others in the Muslim community about being stopped, searched and questioned for hours while returning to New Zealand. My friend Jaballah urged me to come to his local mosque and cover what was going on.

So I followed up. I accompanied him to evening prayers and, just after the sermon, I asked the imam to make a small announcement about the story I was working on. When isha prayers were over, I spoke to no fewer than twenty-five people. A Syrian refugee told me he had been stopped every time he entered the country, and that he was sick of it. A Somali man said his wife was held back for nine hours despite being visibly pregnant, with three children in tow. A young Tunisian man said he'd been stopped on his way back from Sydney, and didn't understand why.

The government at the time shrugged it off, insisting there was no way to determine a person's faith based on their appearance and passport, and hence profiling wasn't happening. The Muslims I had spoken to felt differently.

A year later I saw it first-hand. After flying for twenty-one hours from Turkey to Auckland, my first overseas stint under my belt, I picked up my bags and texted my dad to tell him I had landed. He and my mum waited outside the arrivals gate with a flat white and a 'welcome home' balloon. They'd be sitting outside for four hours, unsure of where I had vanished to, or why I wasn't answering any of their calls.

I'd made it to within twenty metres of where they were standing before a customs officer tapped me on the shoulder in the middle of baggage claim and told me to follow him.

'Come with me. Let's take a shortcut.'

I was sat down on a table to the side of the x-ray machines and the contents of my bags were searched in excruciating detail. I watched as every item was removed and swabbed for bomb residue. My t-shirts. My toothbrush. My underwear. All while passengers looked on in horror as they made their way out to citizenry.

I was presented with a list of every location I had travelled to within the last year, and asked to explain each. Why was I in Israel in September? What business did I have in London in January? My phone and laptop were taken to a hidden room and scanned for an hour, and I was asked to explain photos that piqued interest.

'Why are you standing outside the Dome of the Rock with your finger in the air?'

Each time my phone began to vibrate, and I saw 'Dad' pop up on the screen, the customs agent told me sternly not to touch it. Suddenly I realised that even though I had reported on this exact situation, I didn't really know what my rights were. What did customs practices dictate, and which could I refuse without being arrested?

My New Zealand passport, which had shielded me from dispossession and state repression, and granted me the privilege of unrestricted travel, couldn't protect me here. Between the check-in desk and the gangway, surrounded by overpriced perfumes and mountains of Toblerone, the dignities my parents had migrated to earn suddenly failed me.

What I remember most clearly were the reactions of my fellow travellers, staring as they passed me. A mix of intrigue and surmise that they had stumbled into an episode of *Border Patrol* and would get to see an officer lift a sack of cocaine from the lining of a duffle bag as the music swelled and a sardonic narrator chimed in: 'For this weary-eyed young traveller, looks like the party's over.'

Despite my White-passing face, my blue eyes and my honest intentions, here I was reduced simply to my name, my place of birth and what was left unspoken in the margins. Mohamed Hassan. Born in Cairo. Muslim. Security threat. Suspect. Terrorist. It is a reality magnified for others with darker complexions than mine, with hijabs and kurtas that betray them.

I'm not sure who to blame for all of this—my colleagues in the media and their lust for hyperbole; the politicians lullabyed into the arms of dog-whistle populism; or the perpetrators of the September 11 attacks that have irreversibly changed international travel forever.

What I do know is that the sense of unimpeded adventure that had rushed through my veins each time I stepped into an airport started to fade. I started to dread the superficial niceties of terminal security guards, the passport control clerks with a million questions, the vacuum of time between my passport being scanned and my visa stamped where anything can happen.

I've stopped asking my parents to pick me up from the airport. I walk through terminals with my body tense and a smile I stretch around my ears. It is a mask I wear to protect myself from suspicion. To protect others from fear. I take it off in the bathroom and exhale.

I don't want to think about my identity as a virus. It would break my mother's heart. It is not an inheritance I wish to leave the children I hope one day to have. Instead, it is a story I am retelling in my own words—glumly, humorously, poetically, over and over—until one day it belongs only to me.

8

Ithaka and the lonely god

WHEN ALEXANDER THE GREAT REACHED THE Valley of the Kings in what is now Luxor, he was mesmerised by the temples and complex and intimate burial sites of the Ancient Egyptians. They must have felt as old to him as he feels to us—some of the well-kept temples still alive with colour and stories of mortals ascending to converse with gods.

Alexander had conquered the world and now he too wanted to become a god.

He instructed one of the local high priests to grant him his wish, to decorate him with the promise of immortality, and construct for him a future burial site—a vessel that would one day carry his body to the afterlife, where he would be an equal among past pharaohs and deities. Akhenaton, Osiris, Ra, Alexander.

The priest obliged, understanding it was his only choice, and performed the cleansing ritual. He instructed the local architects to design and construct a small chamber, in the middle of which a square sarcophagus would be built. When it was done, young Alexander stepped into his own grave and wondered what eternity might feel like. In a few months' time, he would go on to conquer Persia, then the kingdoms of India, and in the process he would seal his own fate.

He would die from battle wounds in Mesopotamia before he could return to be buried as a pharaoh.

But what he didn't know, standing with Egypt's finest builders and mystics, is that it wasn't real. The high priest he entrusted with his soul had played a trick on him, indulging the young general in his fantasies, but never with any real intention of worshipping him.

Instead it would be one of his trusted companions, Ptolemy, who would transform him into a deity, though not entirely for altruistic reasons. During a funeral procession that was transporting Alexander back to Macedonia, the body was seized by Ptolemy's forces. It was taken instead to the Egyptian city of Memphis and later to Alexandria, where a new tomb would be built. There, it was claimed the great general had ascended to the realm of the gods and that his half-brother Ptolemy would rule Egypt in his place. (It's highly unlikely Ptolemy and Alexander were actually related by blood, but why let that get in the way of a good propaganda campaign?)

The Ptolemies would continue to rule Egypt for three centuries, building ever more elaborate temples to Alexander and the Egyptian gods. Each generation of structures resembled the ancient tombs that lay before them; each new Ptolemy commanded the people he ruled over to bow before the divinity of the short man from Macedonia. The Ptolemies carried his blood, and were therefore gods themselves.

The last of them was Cleopatra, the only ruler of the dynasty to learn the local Egyptian Cypriotic language. When she committed suicide, Caesarion, her son with Julius Caesar, was sidelined and later executed by his brother-by-adoption Octavian, who was manoevering himself towards power following Caesar's assassination and would soon lead the Roman Empire as Caesar Augustus.

Almost two thousand years later, the French painter Lionel Royer depicted the historic 'meeting' between Augustus and Alexander, whose mummified body was uncovered for the conqueror's visit to Alexandria. The painting exudes reverence, symbolising the transfer of power from the Hellenistic world to the Roman one—though it's said that the former deity's remains were so fragile his nose broke off when Augustus touched it.

In many ways, modern-day Greece resembles Egypt. The cracked and fading Mediterranean pastels of a towering civilisation reduced to a quaint tourist hub where the world's middle classes splash their superior currencies. When tourists marvel at the depth and breadth of the archaeology, the thunderous tales of conquest, science and philosophy that reached for the heavens and mapped the stars and the inner minds of men, the locals smile and nod, indulging their new rulers in their fantasies. They look around at their crumbling lives, carved in the spaces left between history, and marvel at the irony.

The locals hold up the new-age tablets and capture the essence of the foreigners. The tourists grin and pose before the Parthenon or the Pyramids, hoping to immortalise a moment, and by extension themselves, before the world's eye.

Will our greatest of grandchildren unearth our metadata and try and decipher what our selfies said about our civilisation?

Will they realise that, like Alexander, we were just trying to carve out a place in a world that was moving too fast for us?

Perhaps only the descendants of gods, surviving in the economic ashes of these once great cities, understand that none of it is real.

I stand patiently at a café outside the Acropolis Museum, desperate for an iced espresso to shake my soul awake in the midsummer heat. The barista doesn't see me. He sits on a table outside with his face resting on his palms, staring up at the heavens. When he finally notices me, he laughs and apologises.

'I was just staring at this beautiful cloud.'

I look up. It *is* a hell of a cloud. It could've been Olympus Mons itself.

Athens holds a special place in my heart, mostly because it reminds me of Cairo. The nonchalance, the sense of humour, the mischievous kindness in the eye. It seems that we learnt a lot from each other during those 300 years of Ptolemaic rule.

We Egyptians too are descended from greatness but laugh at the suggestion we are somehow still connected to it. Our economies have collapsed, and our people stave off societal malaise. Most taxi drivers can quote poetry to you, sing the songs of the 1930s, talk circles around you about politics and history. Most café baristas have master's degrees, studied to build towers and bridges, wrestled with the justice system, could lay down the blueprints for future worlds. But alas—they, too, sit and stare at the clouds. What else is there to do but dream?

In a cramped cobblestone alleyway embraced by greenery, my eye is captured by a jewellery store in which Ancient Greek poetry is carved into bracelets. Of course I am sucked in, suckered in, and soon the jeweller, Margarita, is sharing with me her favourite passages from the Greek poet Cavafy.

> Laistrygonians, Cyclops,
> wild Poseidon—you won't encounter them
> unless you bring them along inside your soul,
> unless your soul sets them up in front of you.

She tells me all her favourite poems are about the sea. Despite growing up in land-locked Athena, she is drawn to the wild of the Mediterranean. The journey of water. Of finding yourself wherever you are, purging your soul of the monsters who haunt it.

I later find out Cavafy was born and spent most of his life in mystic Alexandria—the city named after one of history's most restless souls, who conquered the world but could not conquer himself. Like me, Cavafy was lost in his own homesickness, spending his career writing on a place he never truly belonged to, yet always longed for. He was born in Egypt, and he died there. For all practical purposes he was Egyptian. And yet somewhere inside him beat this tiny persistent nostalgia for the Greek soil his body never knew.

Like Odysseus, he was flung far from home, desperate to return to an idea in his mind of what that home was. But each time he returns, he finds the landscape altered, the people changed, and his coveted Ithaka a distant memory. Would Alexander have felt the same about his beloved Pella had he found the chance to return from his odyssey? Would he have given up immortality for home?

The poem continues:

> And if you find her poor, Ithaka won't have fooled you.
> Wise as you will have become, so full of experience,
> you'll have understood by then what these Ithakas mean.

I tell Margarita that her city is alive with history, that it hides in every inch of marble, telling its story for all to hear.

'That's interesting,' she says. 'We don't see it.'

9

Always watching

SING WITH ME AN IMMIGRANT'S PRAYER, on nights when the sky is a telescope, opening and closing and peering down into our homes and our subconscious, wide awake.

> I seek refuge in you
> O Allah
> so guide my hand

When I was ten years old, I would stare at the sky through my bedroom window while the world slept. There were messages beaming down from the moon, a golden flute played somewhere in space, sending the faintest vibrations through the atmosphere. Three hundred thousand kilometres away, I sat at the edge of my bed, listening. It was the faintest of sounds, gentle and true, telling me a secret. Tonight would be my last here on earth.

> O Allah
> help me to remember you
> to thank you
> and to serve you well

I would tiptoe out of bed, quietly wash my face, arms and feet in the bathroom sink, and lay out the prayer mat in our dim living room. I didn't really know what I was supposed to do, but I knew I had limited time to do it. I prayed four prostrations, whispering the few verses I knew from the Quran under my breath and held my eyes closed tight. When I was done I sat cross-legged on the mat and lifted my palms to my face. I made a duaa, a supplication, for my sins to be washed away, for my parents to be well, for my brother and sister to be protected. I felt the weight of each word glisten from the corner of my eyes, and my heart expanded and burned.

I folded the prayer mat and returned it to its place on the dining-room chair, then crept back to my bedroom. Along the way, I stopped briefly to see my baby sister Basma one last time. She slept in complete abandon like only an infant can, her fingers curled into themselves and her breath like a moth dancing around a faint sun.

I returned to bed, lifted the sheets to my chin, and watched the moon blow its flute to anyone willing to listen. I pursed my lips and recited what I imagined would be my final words.

    I bear witness
      there is no god but Allah
      and that Muhammad is his messenger

I closed my eyes when sleep finally fell, and slowly my little world began to drift away.

In Sunday school, we were taught by our mothers-turned-volunteer-religious-teachers that in the wee hours of the morning, the layers of heaven contract and God leans in to listen to the prayers of the faithful. Like a shutter's eye pulling focus, the tethered link between the here and the hereafter shrinks, and our mortal wants float up and are embraced. It is why the time just before dawn is so sacred, when worship is most encouraged.

My mother wakes up two hours before dawn each day and prays. By the time we peel our warm bodies from slumber and shuffle into the kitchen with screaming bodies, she has already bested the morning, and laid our sandwiches on the dining table.

Before me and my brother march ourselves through the front door and make the trek to Milford Primary School, my mother straightens the collars on our matching sky-blue polos and farewells us with the Shahada.

'There is no god but Allah.'

'And Muhammad is his messenger,' we mumble robotically as we race down the front steps and back out into the world.

As she closes the door behind us, she whispers a prayer directly to God.

Please watch over my children and steer them clear from harm

As children, we are reminded constantly of the ever-watchful eye above. In times of distress or ease, in anguish and in gratitude, we are told to address Allah using one of his ninety-nine names and trust that nothing escapes his dominion. When we are conspiring with our siblings to commit mischief in the blind spots of our parents, we are reminded that God sees all.

My friend Ken tells students in his poetry classes that because the science of physics dictates that energy never truly disappears, it means that every word ever uttered still exists, its sound floating somewhere in the cosmos, faint but present. In the Quran, God creates the universe with a single word:

Be

And it is. A great unfurling energy that expands rapidly and brilliantly through nothingness. A beginning that curls around itself and spins further and further out. Is that where our prayers go? Are they collected like radio waves on a sensor millions of lightyears away, answered only when our lives have long since passed and our tiny earth is long extinguished? Are they left on hold in a queue of billions while

'Slice of Heaven' plays on a loop down the receiver's end, crackling with distance?

When my parents migrated in 1997, they left behind an Egypt full of watchful eyes. The patriarchal benevolence of Hosni Mubarak's police state insisted on nationalism over religion. In response, the Islamists grew more and more popular at a grassroots level, making the country much more conservative. That was perceived as a threat to the state's ability to control people's public and private behaviours. Since the assassination of President Anwar Sadat in 1981 by fanatical militants who were radicalised in the army's torture chambers, Egypt had been under the continuous martial law of Mubarak's regime. Public gatherings were banned. Protests were banned. Secret police proliferated throughout society, trying to weed out disloyalty.

The most comical of these were the fake fruit-sellers, men with handlebar moustaches and dark-tinted sunglasses who sat on the side of the road next to a cart of stale fruits. The fruits weren't for sale. No one ever asked to buy them. The man stationed there would simply show up each morning and stare at the passers-by until the evening, when he would pack up the cart and wheel it back to the police station. The only place the government couldn't stop people from gathering were the mosques, which would fill up each day with Egyptians of all colours, and on Fridays the worshippers would overflow to the courtyards to pray together and listen to the sermon. But hidden in the crowds were those men with handlebar moustaches, keeping tabs on young people who prayed every day, or attended Quran lessons regularly. If you were young and grew out your beard, you immediately raised suspicions. One day on your way back from the mosque, a paddy wagon might pull up behind you and you would disappear for months. Some people reappeared in mass trials in different districts. Some appeared at the morgue. Some were never found.

It's ironic that we found the freedom to practise Islam openly outside the Muslim world. In New Zealand, no one really knew what Muslims were, why we dressed the way we did, or what our practices were. In tiny community mosques repurposed from auto repair shops and warehouses, we worshipped without looking over our shoulders. My parents instilled in me and my siblings the need to hold tightly on to our identity and taught us to take pride in our beliefs. To pray in public spaces and befriend other Muslims. We held community BBQs in parks and prayed together in large groups, confident that the laws that protected the country's citizens would also extend to us new immigrants.

But soon one ignorance gave way to another. In 2001 the world suddenly became obsessed with Islam, and the quiet space we had to pray was disrupted. The paranoia my family had hoped to escape wormed its way back into our lives. Suddenly wearing a hijab in public became dangerous. Muslim women were abused by passers-by. Some were denied entry on to buses. Having a beard would almost certainly deny you job interviews. A man interrupted me and my friends at Killarney Park in Takapuna, demanding that we stop praying because we 'shouldn't be doing that in this country'. A Syrian friend was told by a prospective employer to change his name or 'no one in their right mind' would want to hire him. My sister was berated in front of her social studies class at the age of thirteen and asked to justify Islamic punitive laws. Even non-Muslims weren't immune. A Sikh man studying at a café outside his medical school had police called to interrogate him after a woman spotted wires hanging out of his bag. They were headphone cables.

The growing mistrust was fuelled by grotesque and irresponsible media narratives that portrayed Muslim immigrants as an existential threat, and the public believed it. Behind the scenes, the same ignorance and fear was spreading in the intelligence community, who now saw their role as guardians of Western civilisation against the threat of Islam. The United States paved the way, building counter-terror networks that scrutinised Muslim communities, infiltrating mosques, tapping phones and blackmailing immigrants into becoming informants. Dozens of Arab and Muslim men were arrested and tried on vague terror charges, from selling bootlegged VHS tapes of Islamic sermons to fundraising for Syrian refugees. Under the language of war, every community endeavour was really a cover-up for sinister plots. A group of Arab students was tried by a US court for operating a 'sleeper cell' in Detroit. The prosecution presented a home video one of them had taken on a visit to Disneyland, claiming it was proof they were scoping out theme park rides as potential targets to plant homemade explosives. NYPD officers used parking tickets to blackmail Muslim New Yorkers into becoming informants. FBI operatives posed as converts and tried to convince community imams to join their 'jihad'. Overseas, hundreds were arrested in CIA black sites and extradited to the Guantánamo Bay detention centre, where they would languish for years without trial or charge, trying to prove their innocence and begging their home countries to take them back.

The new order demanded absolute loyalty from its foes and its friends. Through trade negotiations, the United States ensured its allies would adopt similar counter-terror laws, and most were happy to oblige. Australia sent extra police to Muslim communities; they pulled over Arab kids and checked their IDs. The Australian police ran public terror raids in the heart of Western Sydney, tipping media crews off so they could come and broadcast live outside suburban homes as forces in tactical gear stormed into homes and dragged out confused young men with beards. A decorative sword confiscated from a Lebanese household in Sydney was paraded in front of cameras as proof of a foiled conspiracy. Under Helen Clark, New Zealand detained Algerian asylum seeker Ahmed Zaoui for years in solitary confinement, accusing him, without proof, of links to Al Qaeda. Under John Key, the government gave intelligence agencies sweeping powers of surveillance, allowing them to track and bug phones, computers, airports, homes and mosques. At the same time, repeated pleas from Muslim organisations to meet with the Prime Minister's Office were ignored. The paranoia filled Western societies, and Muslims were left fending for themselves against attacks from every direction. People were suspiciously watching us on the streets, and intelligence operatives were watching us behind closed doors.

In 2010, when Wikileaks published internal memos from US embassies all around the world, we found our Muslim student body, the Auckland University Islamic Society, mentioned in a footnote. The US government was watching our little campus club that held halal sausage sizzles and marriage workshops. Between 2013 and 2015, dozens of young Muslim New Zealanders were approached suddenly by agents of the New Zealand Security Intelligence Service (NZSIS), who made house calls or invited them out for coffee, for a 'casual chat'. I interviewed several members of the Mount Roskill community, some as young as seventeen, who told me they were approached and interviewed without their family's knowledge. They were greeted warmly by affable plain-clothed agents who asked them about their schooling, their families, their problems, before swiftly delving into a string of questions about their social media posts about Syria or Palestine. When these young people couldn't be reached by phone, the agents would turn up suddenly at their homes, sending frantic ripples through families and communities. Some agents, attempting cultural awareness, told Syrian families they were the *mukhabarat*, a word that technically means 'intelligence agents' in Arabic, but is synonymous with the goons that disappeared people in the Middle East.

The families, already hypervigilant about spies and informants sent by the Bashar al-Assad regime to weed out revolutionary sympathisers, were terrified. They would attend rallies of solidarity in Aotea Square wearing masks and balaclavas in fear that photos of their disloyalty would be sent back home and used to round up their parents, cousins and uncles. When the small but historic Shia uprising in Bahrain erupted in 2011, Bahraini international students in New Zealand who gathered in solidarity quickly realised their embassy was keeping notes. Many were blacklisted, their scholarships and visas revoked and their families interrogated. This was the image of *mukhabarat* conjured up in people's minds when the NZSIS showed up.

In 2014 an ad was printed in a local Wellington paper asking for 'community advisors' to come forward and work with NZ intelligence. The ad was written in Somali. It sent shockwaves through the Somali community, leaving its members paranoid and suspicious, accusing each other of being informants. This small, thoughtless advertisement chilled a tiny and defenceless community. Without trusted lawyers, journalists or local politicians to champion their case, they were forced to retreat inwards. Somali travellers were stopped and interrogated at Auckland Airport. A young Somali man was asked if he would report to intelligence officers regularly about what was happening in his community, and in exchange his citizenship application could be fast-tracked.

In 2016 I interviewed a young Libyan man who'd been targeted by NZSIS for recruitment as a paid informant. Two male agents met with him over coffee, and then showed up at his home. They asked him to travel around the country and record information gathered in mosques. In exchange he was offered cash and anonymity. The invitation terrified him.

'When they offered me job offers, I sort of didn't turn it down. I think maybe if I was abrupt with them and shut it down, it would have just been left then and there.'

He was first asked to become a plant at his local mosque in Auckland. When he refused, he was offered a transfer to another part of the country where he could embed himself in the Muslim community there. He refused again, but they persisted.

'Towards the end I got the impression that they were starting to harass me.'

Then they disappeared from his life suddenly, but he was left looking over his shoulder, convinced they were still monitoring him. An elderly woman who approached him outside a mall and asked him to help her change a SIM card on her phone left him spiralling for days, certain she was an agent sent to convey a message to him. He felt like he was losing his mind, and he was certain that he wasn't the only one who'd been approached to spy on the Muslim community. 'They've got informants in the community, and they're watching.'

I joked about it with my friends. We warned each other about speaking too frankly on social media, or on the phone, in case the government was listening.

If someone made an off-colour joke on a WhatsApp thread, it was usually followed by a declarative statement addressed to the silent but watchful other: 'If you're listening, FBI, I didn't really mean that lol.'

In 2013, when Edward Snowden uncovered Five Eyes, a mass surveillance and data-sharing programme that New Zealand spy agencies had signed up to with their partners in the United States, United Kingdom, Canada and Australia, many in the public were outraged. The Muslim community, on the other hand, didn't flinch. We had always assumed we were being watched.

Each time I reported on one of these stories, the government would brush it off, saying there was no real proof any of it was happening. Muslims weren't being unfairly monitored. NZSIS tactics couldn't be discussed because of 'national security concerns'.

When I experienced airport profiling first hand a year later at Auckland Airport, I was shocked at how extensively Customs had documented my travel history abroad. I was monitored when I accepted work deployments as a journalist. I was monitored while vacationing with my brother in Spain.

There's this memory I have from when I was a teenager visiting my family in Cairo. It's of an Egyptian boy being berated by a police officer in the middle of the street. I was with my cousins outside a juice stand, watching the officer slap him across the face several times while demanding to see his government ID, which the boy said he forgot at home. No one stopped to help. No one could. We all stood watching as this humiliated boy was stunned to silence, his big eyes gripped with terror as he came to grips with a lesson about the world he was trapped in. One where self-made gods abased their servants, knowing there are no repercussions to absolute power. In 2011, when the country finally turned against Mubarak's surveillance state, protesters chased down police officers in the street and beat them. The interior ministry was set on fire and burned for days in the heart of the capital. One god had been forsaken, but soon another would take his place.

There were several nights as a kid when I was convinced I would die in my sleep. Afterwards, still breathing, I believed with all my bones that I had been granted a heads-up, a reprieve, in my final moments. I don't know why I felt this with such certainty, but there was a comfort in knowing I wasn't alone here on this strange rock, that an all-powerful presence was watching over me, protecting me from evil, preparing me for the next life. I still sit at the edge of my bed and try to glimpse all of existence in a single frame. Zoom further and further out until all the constellations danced before my eyes, telling a story in perfect ethereal symmetry. Further and further out until I could see the beginning, the *Be* that started it all, and beyond it, the eye that watches.

But is it really God who stares back at us when we gaze at the skies, or the surveillance state, its satellites winking back at us—ever loving, ever watching, a home from which all our efforts to escape cease?

10

Ode to Elliot Alderson

> What if changing the world was just about being here, by showing up, no matter how many times we get told we don't belong?
> —Mr. Robot

WHEN RAMI MALEK SPEAKS ARABIC, HE searches frantically for words. He speaks like an eight-year-old trying to repair the root of a dying tree. He speaks like a cellphone losing signal in a long tunnel. He speaks like me.

I started watching *Mr. Robot* by mistake. Back in 2017, it was an obscure niche show on a network no one had ever heard of. It was weird and punk and anti-capitalist before TikTok had turned all the Zoomers into Marxists. It seemed too good to be true; a high-budget production in the aftermath of the Arab Spring and Occupy Wall Street, proselytising about toxic consumerism and toxic masculinity, preaching to a choir of disillusioned millennials whose future was stolen by their property investor parents who pulled up the ladder before any of them had a chance to dream. It was a show about loneliness and mental illness and drug dependency, years before the glossy hedonism of *Euphoria*, but retaining a beating sincerity that was intoxicating and wounded.

It was only a matter of time before kids on the internet ripped Elliot's monologue from the pilot episode about how capitalism destroyed every genuine notion we still held on to, and how America was an empire built on lies and the bones of third-world children. Then the rest of us started paying attention.

The show's attitudes were all due to the understated genius of Sam Esmail, an Egyptian–American kid from the suburban ghetto of New Jersey, who had dreamt the full world of *Mr. Robot* in its absolute form and pitched the show as a contained five-season arc. There was not a note out of place. Sam was the nerdy perfectionist maestro the internet had been waiting for. But it was Rami Malek's heart-wrenching introversion that grounded the show's daring premise.

I never noticed just how Egyptian he looked until I saw his twin brother, slightly chubbier and unshaven, standing next to him outside the Oscars. Rami was just a cleaned-up version of a makwagy (the man who irons your clothes for you for a couple of pounds, usually on an ironing board outside your apartment block, then brings it up to you at the end of the weekend), with all the intensity of an Egyptian and the quiet of a first-gen immigrant kid thrown into the jaws of primary-school social life with no grasp of English. Yes, I'm projecting, and yes, that's the point. It hurts to finally find representation on screen in your late twenties.

I didn't have an Elliot when I was tumbling through high school. I had Osama bin Laden and the obnoxious and hairy tour guide from the first *Mummy* film played by Persian–British actor Omid Djalili. I rewatched it again recently and was aghast at the nonchalance of its racism. How was this normal for us growing up? How did we not flinch at the cheap jokes, the sea of robed and dusty Arab farmers yelling nonsensically, frothing at the mouth for blood? This is all I had growing up, and I often wonder what damage it did to my self-esteem, to the potential I saw for myself in the world. Who could I become if I couldn't imagine myself outside of these cartoonish stereotypes?

For Malek, it took years of playing background White-passing characters in sitcoms and indie films. His most prominent role before then was as Ahkmenrah in *Night at the Museum*. At least he was Egyptian, right?

But then he was sidelined in the sequel in favour of cultural chameleon and Brown-whisperer Hank Azaria, who spent decades defending his obscene and lazy role as Apu from *The Simpsons*. He helped introduce high-school bullies everywhere to a cheap foreign accent they could imitate for guaranteed laughs at the expense of the poor foreign kid at the back of the class. Soon he was joined by Sacha Baron Cohen's Borat, a caricature which somehow lives on as a respected and canonised example of comic genius and not a profoundly racist lowbrow punch-down. Cohen has carved his entire career on such gags, from his one-dimensional faux satirical appropriation of Black culture in Ali G, to his exhausting and redundant piss-take of the Arab world in *The Dictator*. All his material recycles familiar and tired stereotypes, which he lathers over his skin and dances, plucking cheap laughs at the expense of cultures that never feature in his films or speak with any agency.

I watched the *Borat* sequel with squinted eyes, trying to figure out why a film like this could still be celebrated. Maybe there was some hidden layer that I couldn't grasp. An inside joke that everyone else was getting but me. But I could not find it. And yet Cohen has been lauded as an intellectual for shedding light on Western antisemitism and homophobia, despite dragging other silenced people through the mud to do it. His films allow us to laugh at racist jokes the way we secretly want to, without feeling guilty.

We feel superior to the dumb White Americans he fools into exposing their prejudices, while never being challenged about our own.

The problematic conversation around diversity and representation in film was summed up in a viral interview clip between Matt Damon and Effie Brown from 2015, in which Damon pushed back against the notion that power in Hollywood is concentrated in the hands of White directors, writers and producers, saying that because there were now plenty of actors of colour on screen, it wasn't necessary also to have people behind the camera who weren't White. It was easy for celebrities to champion inclusion, but when their own privileges were highlighted, many of them got defensive.

When Ridley Scott picked an all-White cast in his interpretation of the biblical story of Moses in *Exodus: Gods and Kings,* he justified it by saying there was no way he could finance a film by casting 'Mohamed so-and-so', and that those complaining should 'get a life'. Christian Bale played Moses—opposite Joel Edgerton in a tan as the pharaoh and Sigourney Weaver as the pharaoh's wife. When he was asked why a film that takes place in Egypt failed to employ anyone of Egyptian, North African or Arab descent, he simply responded: 'If people start supporting those films ... then financiers in the market will follow.'

Media mogul Rupert Murdoch jumped in: 'Since when are Egyptians not White? All I know are.'

Despite the rich history of film in Egypt, which served for almost a century as the cultural and entertainment heart of the Middle East, it was too inconvenient to hire Egyptian actors to play main roles, or any role for that matter, in a story ultimately about Egyptian history and mythology. A few years later, Israeli actress and former IDF soldier Gal Gadot was announced in a starring role in an upcoming adaptation of *Cleopatra*. It was billed as a 'feminist film', told from the perspective of the ignored female voice in historical narrative. Without a hint of irony, my own people's history was sidelined once again. Another group of White producers frolicking through other people's cultures, clipping flowers from the shrub, and leaving the roots to rot.

Am I bitter? You bet. Am I surprised? Nope. As a Muslim, I've never had any faith in Hollywood. It is an industry that for decades was the only source of information on Islam and Muslims for billions of people and what they saw were monsters marionetted on screen to sell cinema tickets. Grotesque antagonists screaming nonsensically, cloaked in black, firing AK-47 rifles in the air before getting mowed down by Arnold Schwarzenegger or Sylvester Stallone or Harrison Ford or whatever heroic White saviour was in season that year.

My people, my history, my culture, and my religion were plot points salivated over by film producers in California in writing rooms, shaking each other's hands while making millions off our systematic erasure. When the War on Terror began, this machine went into hyperdrive, bolstered by a 24-hour news cycle that bartered in our misery. We were painted as barbaric hordes of angry men dreaming of violence; humiliated women reduced to Orientalist fantasies, conspirators in their own subjugation; scheming two-faced immigrant communities aiming terror at the heart of Western civilisation.

For decades, this was the image of Muslims anyone saw. For decades, this was the image Muslim immigrants saw of ourselves. We were raised on it, and so was everyone else. Meanwhile, the true toll of war and counter-terrorism was destroying nations, ripping apart communities and leaving Muslim minorities to fend for themselves against the overwhelming whirlpool of hatred, fear and paranoia swirling around us. We were entirely alone, vulnerable and denied even the right to speak for ourselves.

This is why *Mr. Robot* means so much, because true representation lies in authenticity, regardless of where it stems from. I watched the Korean–American film *Minari* and felt seen by it. *Black Panther* was universally adored, not just by the African diaspora. There is a magic in telling your own story proudly and without fear, bringing your people with you and giving them licence to shine. *Four Lions* was a comedy about four wannabe terrorists made by a White director, but it captured so much nuance from the Muslim community that we celebrated it, a story that took the time to understand its characters and didn't tokenise them.

When Elliot walks into a mosque in a self-contained episode in New Jersey, he's told to take his shoes off at the door, which he does. It is these delicate brush strokes that paint a fuller picture. When the hijab-wearing hacker Trenton joins Elliot's team of ragtag revolutionaries, we see her praying and taking care of her parents, while skateboarding and chasing love interests. These aren't contradictions, they're layers.

These are the kinds of storytellers we need, the roles we need to see ourselves in. When I was eight years old, chasing my friends around the school playground, I wasn't imagining I was the brooding out-of-focus Muslim extra, blood lustful and menacing. I was Enzo Matrix from *ReBoot*, I was Hercules, the blue Power Ranger, TJ from *Recess* (and sometimes Spinelli), Michelangelo from *Teenage Mutant Ninja Turtles*, Gohan, Ash Ketchum, Doug, Spanky from *Little Rascals*, Neo from *The Matrix*, Ace Ventura and Captain Planet. I was the main character.

It was Hollywood that taught me to sideline myself, to shrink in shame so that no one mistook me for the bad guys on TV. But I didn't deserve that. I deserved to be seen, and to see myself in my best image, to dream of a world with a place for me in it. For a hero who looks like me, speaks with a weird accent like me and has a name that sounds like mine to be celebrated, championed and loved on the widescreen. To think of myself as someone deserving of admiration, who was allowed to believe in himself—to believe he too could take down evil corporations, free his people, and one day save the world.

11

How to be a Bad Muslim

> Either you are with us, or you are with the terrorists.
> —George W Bush

TEN DAYS BEFORE CHRISTMAS ON A steamy midsummer afternoon in 2014, I walked into work for my late shift at TVNZ with my news senses aflame.

I had been working on the assignments desk in Auckland for close to two years. It was a foot in the door of the industry I'd been wanting to join ever since I'd completed my postgraduate diploma in journalism. When popular uprisings roared across the Arab World in 2011 and Al Jazeera journalists became household names, I abandoned my predestined path through Engineering and journeyed to the frontlines of storytelling, much to my parent's horror. The media felt like my calling, a path that stretched out before me illuminated by promise, one where I could finally change the harmful narratives about my community, my religion, my people.

But today was not one of those days. Two thousand kilometres away, an angry man had holed himself up in a Sydney café on Martin Place, holding eighteen innocent people hostage. It was frightening news to wake up to, and it felt close and familiar. I had sat inside the Lindt Chocolate Café myself just six months earlier, while visiting friends in Australia. It was surreal seeing it now live on TV.

In the first hours of the attack, there was little information about who the gunman was and what he wanted. He was an immigrant. He was likely Muslim. That was enough for conclusions to be drawn. Immediately, TV reporters around Australia began speculating about links to ISIS, the mosque he had been radicalised in, and whether there were more attacks planned around the city. All public transport lines were shut down. Schools and office blocks were evacuated. Sydney became a ghost town, except for those two blocks surrounding the café. By noon, every major news outlet in the world was stationed just outside the police cordons, beaming live to the satellites, to a world watching.

It was soon dubbed the 'Sydney Siege'. For sixteen hours, heavily armed police surrounded the café. Almost every vantage point of Martin Place could be seen by flicking through different channels. All except one: inside. Inside was a locked box, and for the entire day all people could do was speculate.

If you've been inside a television newsroom then you know how many screens are around. Dozens tuned to every channel of interest, local and international, at all times. Broadcasters need to be abreast of everything that is happening at all moments, waking and sleeping. If something breaks, they need to already be halfway through writing their initial copy. The BREAKING NEWS ticker must be programmed and ready to go, the studio hastily cleared and sound checks completed. Then *Shortland Street* or *Police Ten 7* will be rudely interrupted to go live to a news anchor with a solemn but professionally approachable face. The tone will be calm, detached, reliable. The music sting urgent but not alarming. What you are about to hear is the most important event happening right now, and you'd best pay attention.

That day in 2014, New Zealand media abandoned its allotted programmes and broadcast coverage of the siege live throughout the entire day. It made sense: it was Australia, our neighbour and reluctant older sibling. Almost all of us had family or friends in Sydney. I thought about Ahmed and Ayman, who I'd visited earlier that year, who lived just a kilometre away in Darling Harbour.

I messaged Ayman:

'Hey habibi. Is everything okay? Are you safe?'

He replied shortly after:

'Yeah man, it's crazy. Everything is shut down. I was at work but they told us all to go home.'

Once I was sure he and his brother were fine:

'Bro, do you wanna go on *One News* and talk about what's going on around you? We're trying to find Kiwis caught up in Sydney right now.'

'Sure.'

I was still on the bus, mentally preparing myself for the start of a gruelling shift during which anything could happen.

When I arrived at the TVNZ complex, I looked up at the sprawling glass panes running the length of the building, opaque enough to hide all but a rush of bodies inside. There was always something important happening inside, but today it might as well have been the centre of the country. This work felt important. I scanned myself in, greeted the same security guard I'd shared the quiet evening with the day before, and walked through the pastel corridor and into the open doors of the newsroom. My heart was racing.

It was even more surreal than I'd imagined. Every television screen across the open workspace, including the six hanging high above the producers' desks in the centre of the room, was tuned to the same thing. Every computer had the live broadcast running on one screen, with the CoStar interface being furiously typed into on the other. All of them were showing the exact same image: the Lindt café, surrounded by special forces stationed at strategic points along the initial cordon, their rifles pointed at the windows and doors. Behind them, armed police held the line on the second cordon, cornered by station wagons. A handful of police dogs wearing stab-proof vests were gathered by the back of one van, standing by for their mission. Beyond them, a flock of reporters and TV cameras made use of all the available space to get as close as they could to the heart of the action. The afternoon sun splashed across one half of the street, splitting the scene into light and dark.

In the top-right-hand corner of the screen, framed by a thin white border, was a mugshot of Man Monis, the Iranian-born Australian man inside with eighteen hostages.

I stood for a second in the doorway, taking it all in, then I stepped inside towards my desk.

And that's when the atmosphere in the room shifted, rupturing along the seams.

One by one, they all looked up from their screens to see me. One by one, their faces went white. First the producers of the evening news desk, then the reporters, then the cameramen, then the shift manager. A blanket fell over the newsroom and no one spoke.

I walked forward, confused at the reaction, wondering if I'd just missed an update. Had a hostage been killed? Was there a second attack? What had happened?

The moment passed, and I took my seat and dived into work, searching up stringers in Sydney we could call in to film for us, checking the statements coming through from Australian police, keeping an eye on the fire scanners in case anything broke closer to home. For the rest of the shift, no one talked to me. When I went to the kitchen to heat up dinner, people avoided my gaze and busily stirred their coffees. I gave the live producers Ayman's number, and they spoke to him on air about the transport shutdowns and the mood of the city. They thanked me politely and ended the conversation.

I tried to not let it get to me, to busy myself with work until the day was over and I could leave, but I couldn't help feeling like my presence was weighing on everyone around me.

I felt like an intruder in a space I had worked in for close to two years. I tried to defuse the tension by asking questions, suggesting story ideas or people I knew who could be willing to talk. It didn't help; I was the tension.

When my shift was over and I was sitting in the work-subsidised taxi back to my parents' house, I played the events over in my head, trying to find an alternative explanation to the one in my gut. The one I was trying not to believe:

My colleagues, these people I worked alongside every day, and whom I desperately wanted to impress, were terrified of me.

The moment I walked through the door, they had looked up from an image of a Muslim man committing an act of extreme violence to see another Muslim man enter their space. Their space. And they were caught off guard, defenceless and vulnerable. In that moment, even if just for a second, they believed I was the same as the man in Martin Place.

Later that night, Australian police stormed the café and shot Man Monis dead. In the process, he shot and killed one of the hostages, the café manager Tori Johnson, and another, lawyer Katrina Dawson, was killed by a ricochet bullet from a police rifle. Investigations into Monis found he had a lengthy and violent police record, accused of over forty counts of sexual assault and of being involved in the murder of his ex-wife. He was diagnosed with schizophrenia by a psychologist. He had been involved in disputes with various mosques and was ostracised from most of them. Days before the attack, he pledged his loyalty to the Islamic State on his personal website, but he had previously claimed to be a spiritual healer, an Iranian intelligence operator, an outlaw bikie and for a while ran under the moniker Ayatollah Mohammed Manteghi Boroujerdi. Eighteen people, including a number from the Muslim community, had alerted the police to his online behaviour, but nothing had been done.

In the days that followed, Martin Place became a memorial for the two victims of the hostage crisis. Family and friends, strangers, schools and community groups visited the café, laying flowers and messages of love on the ground outside the remaining cordons. Soon the entire square became a field of flowers, bringing a hushed silence over the once bustling business hub. Services were held in the two nearby churches, and other Lindt cafés across the city opened their doors to members of the public wishing to pay their respects.

The Muslim community banded together and held funeral prayers at Lakemba Mosque, inviting people from all faiths inside. They scheduled interviews with every TV station that would have them to condemn the attack, condemn violence, condemn ISIS, affirm their commitment to Australia and the Australian way of life.

Still, they were accused of saying nothing. Right-wing shock jocks took to the airwaves to demand more. Muslim spokespeople were asked to publicly condemn ISIS each time they were interviewed, and they did so again and again. Prime Minister Tony Abbott railed against the country's lax immigration and security policies, vowing to tighten the vice on citizenship and counter-terrorism laws and put Australia at the forefront of this new crusade against the 'death cult' of Islamic extremism. He accused the Muslim community of failing to prove they stood for Australian values and that they didn't secretly support the acts of terror they were watching on the news: 'I've often heard Western leaders describe Islam as a "religion of peace". I wish more Muslim leaders would say that more often, and mean it.'

Two months later, my friend Asmaa was out with her mother and sister attending a theatre show in central Sydney, when three men began pelting them with eggs in a parking lot. When they hid inside their car, the men threw something harder, shattering the car's mirror.

Asmaa called the police and reported the incident, but nothing eventuated. That year the Australian Islamophobia Register recorded thousands of incidents of verbal and physical attacks against primarily young Muslim women. In one incident, a woman wearing a hijab was thrown off a train.

Through 2015, dozens of far-right anti-Islamic groups began holding rallies across the country. Groups like Reclaim Australia and the True Blue Crew marched through the streets and demanded an end to 'Muslim migration'. A number of politicians joined them, including Pauline Hanson, who announced her return to politics during a national campaign tour titled 'Fed Up'.

A year later, her party, One Nation, secured 9 per cent of the Queensland vote in the federal election, and she returned triumphantly to the Senate, opening her maiden speech with the words: 'We are in danger of being swamped by Muslims, who bear a culture and ideology that is incompatible with our own.' She called for a ban on Muslim migration, a further tightening of Australia's viscid refugee policy, and a closure of mosques around the country.

Two months after that, Donald J Trump was elected the 45th president of the United States of America. His first order of business in office was signing that executive order shutting down all travel from seven Muslim-majority countries until his administration could 'figure out what the hell is going on'.

While anti-Muslim sentiment has existed since the time of the Crusades, it became entrenched in the public's imagination in the aftermath of the September 11 attacks. At the time, anyone appearing Muslim was a target. Mosques were set on fire in the United States, Australia and New Zealand. Men and women were attacked in the streets, on public transportation. Suffocating counter-terror legislations were passed under urgency to grant governments wartime powers to surveil and wiretap mosques and individuals suspected of harbouring extremist views.

It was never quite clear what those views entailed. Was being angry about the invasion of Iraq and having sympathy for the Palestinian cause grounds for suspicion? In many cases, it was.

News crews followed the flimsiest leads and investigated community events and prayer spaces. When a dispute over the management of Masjid Umar in Mount Roskill escalated to a fight inside the mosque, it was on the front cover of the *New Zealand Herald* the next day. That evening, live television crews broadcast from outside its gates talking about a 'fatwa' that had been passed.

When young Somalis began selling khat—a chewing tobacco-style drug classified as class C in New Zealand but widely used in East Africa—near Hamilton Jamia Mosque, reporters went undercover to investigate the mosque itself. I'll never forget the 'exclusive' footage obtained by TV3 of the Muslim community praying inside the mosque on Friday, captured on a fisheye lens attached to a hidden camera one of the journos snuck inside during prayer time.

Bewildered community leaders were asked to come on TV and defend these events against the suspicions levelled against them by the public. There was nothing they could say that made the situation better. Either they dismissed them as ridiculous stories and looked guilty, or they apologised and looked even guiltier. It was a trap.

Islamic studies professor Yassir Morsi describes the way the language of Islam became weaponised under the War on Terror. Words that were once harmless suddenly took on sinister meanings. 'Fatwa' stopped being a word that meant an Islamic ruling on anything from brushing your teeth correctly to applying for a mortgage with interest rates. Now it was synonymous with targeted assassinations. 'Sharia law' went from being a tautological phrase that literally translates to 'Law law' in Arabic—describing any and all Islamic jurisprudence that includes the entire history of scholarship dating back 1400 years, and details rules of welfare, penal codes and health—to a catchphrase used by dog-whistling politicians. They used the term to warn their constituents of secret plots to destabilise Western legal frameworks and impose medieval courts where women could be hanged for showing skin. Eleven US states passed laws protecting against the implementation of foreign laws, highlighting in particular the dangers of 'creeping Sharia' infiltrating American life through Muslim communities.

The word 'jihad' has by far been the most popular, becoming a favourite for journalists and Hollywood screenwriters. They use it to conjure up a caricature of a balaclava-clad Muslim man with an AK-47, driven by an all-consuming desire to bring an end to Western civilisation. Insurgents in Afghanistan fighting against US occupying forces were called 'jihadis', for example. Some of those same fighters or 'mujahideen' were proudly described as 'freedom fighters' in the 1980s when they were fighting against Russian occupying forces with financial backing from the United States and its Western allies. The word simply means 'struggle' in Arabic, and is used to describe everything from fighting to fasting to financially supporting your parents when they get old.

In a narration from the Prophet Muhammad, he's quoted as telling his companions upon returning from battle with a neighbouring tribe and resuming their normal lives as farmers, bankers and merchants: 'We are finished with the lesser jihad; now we are starting the greater jihad.'

But there was no room for nuance in the media. No one ever sat down with Muslims to understand what our beliefs actually were, or how these concepts were practised in our daily lives. When the go-to labels became overused, the media found inventive ways to pair them up with other menacing words for effect. Islamist jihadist militants. Pro-Sharia radical activists. Salafist-Jihadist extremists. Fatwa-fuelled homegrown ventriloquists. (Okay, I made that last one up, but it still sounds menacing, right? You can play along at home.)

As Morsi writes in the essay collection *I Refuse to Condemn*, the very word 'Muslim' has been hijacked by the language of the War on Terror and contorted into something new. Something darker, more twisted, and further and further removed from how Muslims saw themselves.

Two categories now existed in the public narrative for how Muslims were described: the Good Muslim and the Bad Muslim.

The Good Muslim was moderate. They had toned-down beliefs, didn't take the Quran too seriously, and believed in the enlightened values of the Western world. They waved the flag, hosted BBQs every summer with their neighbours, cheered on their local sports team and cried when the national anthem played. They left the trauma of their countries of birth behind them and embraced whole-heartedly the new world they were now endlessly grateful to have been invited to join. They spoke fluent English, shook hands with their female coworkers and didn't force their wives to wear the headscarf. They were essentially invisible.

On the other side of the coin was the dark, mysterious and troublesome Bad Muslim. They hated their adoptive societies, harbouring resentment and wishing ill on their neighbours. Despite their outward law-abiding nature, they secretly wished for the demise of Western values, believing them to be anti-Islamic and hence in need of a 'jihad'. Unlike their fluffier counterparts, they carried their past traumas with them, refusing to tame their backward and violent natures despite being accepted into a more peaceful and educated world. They were out for blood, waiting for an opportunity to strike at the heart of middle-class suburban life.

More than a billion and a half people around the world were suddenly separated into two distinct groups, regardless of their language, their culture, their history or even the school of Islam they adhered to. You were either with us, or you were with the terrorists.

But that wasn't enough. Under the War on Terror, it now became the job of the Good Muslim to fight the Bad Muslim. To weed them out of their mosques and communities, turn them over to authorities. As Hillary Clinton put it during a 2016 election debate: 'We need American Muslims to be part of our eyes and ears on our front lines.'

It was a polite way of saying what Tony Abbott had said a year earlier; it expressed the ultimate pitfall of this binary. It was no longer enough for Muslim citizens to be good members of their societies. They now had to prove their loyalty to their country, their government, the world. Like a gang recruit in a hazing process desperate to earn their patch, the Muslim was now in the impossible position of being both suspect and informant. If we weren't speaking up, then we were part of the problem. Then we were guilty.

Just like that, the two categories started bleeding into one. The War on Terror twisted our identities yet again, and forced us into a hall of mirrors, all of them distorted, all of them terrifying. In fact, the logic followed, it is the Good Muslim that hides the Bad Muslim's intentions.

Even when we were apologising and condemning every act of violence that happened anywhere in the world, whether we were asked to or not, we were still guilty. The narrative now ran that every Muslim, no matter how innocent, was secretly hiding violent intentions. If Islam was a violent ideology, then it followed that every Muslim was capable of violence. The more 'Muslim' you were, the more dangerous.

The new narrative declared that Islam and all its followers were working together like a hive mind to bring about a new world order: one ruled by Sharia law and the oppression of women; one that would not rest until it brought about the destruction of the 'Judeo–Christian way of life'. Every Muslim was a part of the problem. Every Muslim was hiding something.

To quote New Zealand's former deputy prime minister Winston Peters in his now-infamous 2005 speech aptly titled 'The End of Tolerance': 'These two groups, the moderate and militant, fit hand and glove everywhere they exist ... these groups are like the mythical Hydra—a serpent underbelly with multiple heads capable of striking at any time and in any direction.'

And so we Muslims stood between two images of ourselves, neither of which we had a hand in crafting. Both were guilty. Both required constant apology.

This resulted in a constant state of unease in the way our societies, our media and our governments now dealt with us. It is always there, unspoken, beneath the skin of every interaction. My friend Hassan Raslan once described it as the layer that lies behind every argument with a stranger: 'I can't remember a single conflict I had with anyone, where it didn't eventually turn racist.'

Once he cut someone off in traffic, and was told: 'Go back to your own fucking country, you fucking Muslim.'

This reality is further exacerbated for women, particularly those wearing the headscarf and thus visibly Muslim. Statistics by Islamophobia watchdogs worldwide have consistently shown that Muslim women bear the brunt of attacks, from verbal harassment in public spaces like supermarkets and buses to cowardly physical attacks on the street and blatant discrimination in workplaces.

In Shakira Hussein's book *From Victims to Suspects: Muslim Women Since 9/11*, she examined how this trend shifted over the past twenty years. In the aftermath of the September 11 attacks, the overarching narrative of Muslim women was that of subjugated and silenced minorities who were victims of their radicalised and backward-minded patriarchs.

Intriguingly, Hussein found that as Muslim communities became more integrated into Western societies, and Muslim women became more visible in public roles, whether in high-ranking work positions or represented on screen in the news and in film, this attitude of sympathy began to transform into mistrust and menace. Muslim women were now perceived as more of a threat to society than men, and became the new targets of hate-fuelled attacks.

This can be seen reflected in public policy in countries where anti-Muslim rhetoric has a lot of political sway. France banned headscarves in public schools in 2004 and the niqab in 2010; and the burkini (the Islam-adherent swimsuit) has been banned since in several French cities and resorts. These bans remained in place during the pandemic, when it became mandatory for faces to be covered at all times. The irony wasn't lost on Muslim women.

Partial bans on the headscarf and burka have also been legislated in a number of other European countries, including Germany, the

Netherlands, Belgium, Denmark, Austria, Latvia, Sweden, Bulgaria and Kosovo. In 2021, a top European Union court ruled in favour of workplaces dismissing employees on the grounds that their headscarves were causing tension.

But these bans aren't limited to Western countries. From the 1980s up until 2013, Turkey had one of the world's most stringent hijab bans, outlawing them from public schools, universities and government buildings. Women could not set foot inside public institutions while wearing a headscarf, and those seeking education had to abandon their practice or travel abroad to study in more tolerant institutions. For years, women from traditional Turkish communities protested the ban, only to be met by fierce police crackdowns. Footage from this period shows elderly women pulled and dragged by their scarves through courthouse hallways, their hijabs ripped off and thrown on the ground. Teachers were encouraged to report on their pupils if they attended class while covering their hair, even with a hoodie or a jacket, and many accused educational institutions of lowering their end-of-year grades as punishment.

During the 1990s, as a form of rebellion, some women began wearing wigs on top of their headscarves to bypass the restrictions. This practice became so popular that many class photos from the era show rows of young women seated with identical jet-black bowl cuts.

The wearing of hijab, like all forms of Islamic public practice, was seen by Turkey's military rulers as a violation of the country's strictly secular imperatives. To avoid falling foul of the rules, religious young men serving their mandatory army service would sometimes resort to taking off their pants while praying, in case their peers noticed creases at the knees and reported them to their superiors.

In 1999 the first hijab-wearing MP, Merve Kavakçı, was elected to Parliament. But when she entered to attend her swearing-in ceremony, members from the dominant Democratic Left Party (DSP) banged on their desks for forty-five minutes in protest, while yelling at her, 'Get out! Get out!' Bülent Ecevit, the Turkish prime minister at the time, stood at the parliamentary podium and joined in.

'Put this woman in her place,' he yelled.

Kavakçı later described her sheer terror, saying her heart was about to leap from her chest.

The restrictions, and the public's attitudes, eased over time. The ban was eventually removed fully in 2013, under the new rule of the conservative AK Parti and their charismatic leader, Recep Tayyip Erdoan.

Other Muslim-majority countries mimicking European enlightenment, like Tunisia, also imposed sweeping controls over the attire of women, only overturned by popular democratic revolts like those seen during the Arab Spring. Softer, unspoken bans, on hijabi women and bearded men, were carried out in public institutions, on television and in sports teams right across the Muslim world for decades. When Muslim Brotherhood political figure Mohamed Morsi was elected to the presidency in Egypt in 2012, a year after the secular dictatorship of Hosni Mubarak was toppled, media commentators mercilessly mocked his wife for wearing the hijab. She was called 'uncultured', 'low class' and a 'diplomatic embarrassment' to the image of the country abroad.

My sister Basma once told me wearing the hijab in New Zealand had become exhausting. It felt to her like a full-time job, one she could never clock off from as long as she was outside and visible. When she caught the bus, she could feel the eyes of passengers boring into her neck. If one of them turned around and confronted her, she knew no one would come to her aid. When she started a new job, she'd have to work double time to be the most cheerful and approachable person there to counteract the assumptions written on her colleague's faces as she walked in. She didn't feel entitled to a bad day, to be angry or upset in public lest she allow others the smugness of confirming their beliefs about her.

As long as she wore it around her face, she would be judged for all of her actions by both Muslims and non-Muslims. Was she Muslim enough? Was she too Muslim? Good or Bad? The answer depended on whom you were speaking to.

'I'm tired of always having to smile and be happy so that people don't think I'm a terrorist.'

When I was younger I would walk through the mall with my mother and sister and watch people's faces when we passed them. Most people looked twice. Some with surprise. Some with horror. Others with disgust. People generally tried to hide their reactions, or quickly looked the other way. Some were shameless, staring openly from their food court tables, or nodding to their friends in agreement while their eyebrows arched in disapproval.

It was hard not to feel like a zoo animal, whose purpose was to serve the curious eye of gawkers. They marvelled at this foreign species that had entered their world. Didn't we look so strange, plucked from our African wilderness?

When I caught them doing this I would stare back. Beam my eyes into theirs until they looked away. It was the only thing I could do, to make them feel a small sense of discomfort. Maybe then they'd get it.

My earliest memory of a confrontation is from just months after we'd migrated to New Zealand. The beachy and affluent North Shore suburb of Milford was much less diverse in the 1990s than it is today, and my family stood out like a peacock in a pet store. Mum had just arrived at the supermarket and was circling the parking lot looking for a spot. When we finally found a space, we heard incessant car horns and muffled yelling from behind us. As my mum was taking off her seatbelt and opening the car door, a woman came jousting in from the driver's side, swinging her finger wildly in the air, her face red behind her black sunglasses.

'Sorry, I didn't see you—' my mother attempted, but the words never landed. The woman had already loaded hers and was ready to fire.

'Why don't you just go the hell back to where you came from?'

I don't think my brother and sister, just five and two at the time, remember this incident. It's etched into my memory with unusual clarity. The woman storming back to her car, shaking with self-righteous anger. The onlookers staring with their mouths open. My mother looking ahead without speaking, as she gathered us from the back seat and walked into the Woolworths as if nothing had happened.

In the aftermath of the Christchurch terror attacks in 2019, despite the outpouring of support from the government and the public, the flowers left outside mosques around the country, the TV reporters who donned the hijab in solidarity, the number of anti-Muslim attacks actually rose. I say 'despite', but part of me feels that it's really *because* of all these things. The sudden visibility of Muslim faces on people's televisions in a country that barely saw Muslim New Zealanders outside of news reports about ISIS and the occasional Sonny Bill Williams profile drove many to anger. This wasn't the country many Kiwis were used to, and they weren't happy with how things were changing around them.

The attacks that came after were vicious and targeted, and those in the crosshairs were none other than the people who'd been most affected by the tragedy. Al Noor Mosque, where forty-four worshippers were killed, received multiple threats both online and by phone in the two years that followed the attacks on March 15. At least two people have been charged with threatening violence against the mosque; and in 2021 police began investigating after a photo was uploaded on the online forum 4chan showing a balaclava-clad man sitting in a car outside the mosque. The image was also shared on Telegram more than 2000 times, and was uploaded just two weeks before the second anniversary.

Even the imam, Gamal Fouda, wasn't safe. The man who was leading the Friday sermon during the first attack and watched his own community slaughtered in front of his eyes, and who just a week later led a public prayer with the Muslim community outside the mosque and in front of the world, was still a target. During an election campaign visit to Christchurch, Prime Minister Jacinda Ardern was walking with Fouda and other members of the Muslim community, when a man emerged from the crowd and began berating the imam and those around them, yelling anti-Muslim statements and telling them to 'go home'.

Two months later, the mother and sister of one of the March 15 victims were verbally attacked while shopping in a department store. Aya Al-Umari, whose brother Hussein had stood up to the mosque shooter before losing his life, said a woman and her husband walked past her and her mother Janna while they were picking out lipstick and murmured a comment. When Aya asked them to repeat it, the woman scoffed and told her husband, loud enough so it was clearly audible: 'It's okay, it won't be long before they leave our country.'

The incident, filmed on Aya's phone, went viral, watched and shared by millions of people outraged and shocked that this would happen. But Muslims weren't surprised. This is what we assume people think and feel around us all the time.

It's exhausting. It's infuriating. But what is the recourse? What can we do to stem this irrational fear that we haven't already tried?

We condemn every terror attack that happens, loudly in the media and online. We become successful and thriving members of our societies. We wave the New Zealand flag at rugby games. We build bridges, metaphorical and literal. We save lives in hospitals. We speak in Parliament about social cohesion. We perform poetry at national events. But all this only seems to give those addicted to rage the fuel to feed their bitterness. If our invisibility had left us defenceless, our visibility made us targets.

By the way, Aya and Janna weren't wearing headscarves that day at the department store. They were targeted because they were different; their skin and tongue were enough to make them guilty.

It is a peculiar type of gaslighting, to be subjects of this strange attraction. To be granted citizenry and promised equality but to always be held at arm's length. To be accused of plotting disharmony when all we have ever fought for was integration, acceptance, peace. To be slandered and caricatured by voices that hold all the power and be expected to show gratitude. To be Good Muslims, expected to twirl on command and jump through hoops for an audience of our peers, colleagues and country, proving our loyalty. To be reminded constantly of how lucky we are to have snatched the golden ticket to escape our oppressive and backward homes, only to be asked to remain obedient and silent. Be grateful. Be the model minority. Be quiet.

Winston Peters never apologised for his racist speech, nor the repeated fear-mongering he spread about the Muslim community for a leg-up at election time. He was forgiven for it, the way his anti-Asian rhetoric always was, in part because many people believed what he was saying to be true. That no matter how Good they may seem, Muslims were not to be trusted.

My parents often warned me about attending protests and speaking out, about writing politically charged poems and reporting on racial profiling in our community. They tell me it's this country's right to be suspicious. That we are foreigners and will always be seen that way. It is a practice of survival that many first-generation immigrants understand. That I, as an idealistic third-culture child desperate for belonging, but having been shielded from the worst tolls of xenophobia, cannot truly grasp.

But it is this privilege I am afforded that gives me a sense of entitlement to equality. This country is all I know, and I'll be damned if I'm asked to jump through another hoop or dance for a mob to distract them, to take their minds off the ways I affront their way of life. I no longer care about making people feel uncomfortable, even if it goes against all of my wiring. I cannot keep shrinking. I cannot keep cutting out parts of my identity so that I may take up less space, be harmless and polite and overlooked. I can't do this anymore. I am tired. We all are tired.

The day of the Sydney Siege left me shaken for a long time. It was the first moment I realised that in some people's eyes, I would never be more than a 'Muslim'. I could attempt to be agreeable, but there would always be a barrier, a lens through which I would be analysed and judged. That when it really came down to it, there was never really a place for me in 'us'.

During an appraisal meeting at TVNZ later that year, I was told I was being passed over for promotion because I wasn't showing enough initiative. I was too quiet, and it was hard to tell whether I was competent at my job. It was the third time I'd been told this; the third time I watched my peers overtake me despite my attempts at proving myself.

I internalised it then, wondering if I had made a huge mistake in going to journalism school. Maybe I wasn't cut out for this. Maybe I should quit.

But looking back now, ten years into my career, having met and worked alongside so many supportive and open people, I realise the problem wasn't me. The truth was that some of the people around me then had made up their minds about who I was the moment I'd stepped through the door on my first day, and they were unwilling to change them.

Most importantly, I realise that wasn't my burden to bear. I have to live my life without apologising for it, without negotiating my existence with anyone. There is simply no other alternative.

And I guess that makes me one of the Bad ones.

12

The curse of the Bosphorus Strait

WHEN I WAS LIVING IN ISTANBUL, I had this theory I kept annoying my friends with. It was an elaborate explanation as to why we strangers had been brought to this strange land, and what we were expected to do.

We were working for the Turkish broadcaster, but most of us were from far-flung places like Atlanta and Nairobi and Auckland. We were a community of expats suddenly thrown into an environment where no one from outside our office spoke English. None of us spoke a lick of Turkish.

I tried, desperately, to learn. I spent two hours a day on Duolingo piecing adjectives together in what felt like a giant jigsaw puzzle with no box to compare the final image to. It seemed that my cerebral cortex had thrown in the towel after learning English, which is hugely embarrassing whenever I meet journalists who know at least five languages. Being bilingual as a third-culture kid is no bragging right, and I had moved to a city that thought little of my forked tongue.

In Istanbul, the ancient stone moulds its arms over you as you sleep, and soon you are embroidered in its fabric. You ride the ferry between Asia and Europe and drink the salted Bosphorus air. You pour distilled tea over your bones after every meal and conversation to survive another icy January. You fight over fudged toll meters with bitter taxi drivers, the necessary antagonists streaming through the city's arteries.

One tried to run me over once when I refused to pay double the fare while going to meet friends for breakfast. We screamed at each other in different languages until I hurled money on the dashboard and threw the door shut behind me. He slammed the gears into reverse and gassed it as I walked around his car to get to the restaurant. It was a Sunday morning.

I spent three years in a foreign country with no exit strategy, knowing enough local words not to starve. Like almost everyone I met, I'd arrived on a whim, through an unexpected email or phone call, a whiff of mystery caught in the afternoon air. I was looking for the next stage in my career as a journalist, that was true. But I was also looking for my own escape. I had spent most of my life living on an island, looking out to the rest of the world in yearning. It was time to swim out and seek fortune and adventure.

My unexpected call came in the form of an intrepid journalist I crossed paths with by accident or serendipity. I met Yasmine Ryan in 2016 when she walked into our office at Radio New Zealand one morning without any fanfare, picking up casual shifts in between flashier gigs abroad: *Al Jazeera, The Independent, The New York Times, The World Press Institute*. I had pored over her work and heard stories from my Tunisian friends about how she was one of the first foreign journalists to cover the uprising against Ben Ali in 2010–11, and how she didn't cover it like a White reporter. To a young journo with his eyes on the Middle East, Yasmine may as well have walked in with a cape and a rush of wind.

We drove to Ormiston Primary School to cover an announcement by the deputy minister of education about investing in charter schools. I was tasked with showing her how to work the ancient RNZ mics and not much else. We made small talk with Nikki Kaye about her cat after we accidentally broke the pen the school was about to gift her, and then drove back to the office and filed a story no one remembered. It wasn't the Arab Spring.

A few weeks later, Yasmine messaged me to give me a heads up about a front-page feature she was filing for the *Weekend Herald* about young Muslims being interrogated by Customs at Auckland Airport. She knew I'd been covering the topic and wanted to give me the courtesy of knowing when her story would go live. It was a tiny beautiful gesture only someone who truly believed in the craft would make.

That was the end of our interaction, until I received an early-morning Facebook message from her asking if I was still interested in a stint at an international newsroom. Would I consider moving to Turkey? I couldn't believe it.

Four months later, in May 2017, I meet Yasmine at a café in Cihangir, a leafy expat neighbourhood that once belonged to Istanbul's rich and powerful artists and still retained a quirky edge of gay rights activism and middle-class bohemia. The vibe was similar enough to the anarchist counterculture of Karangahape Road for me to feel I belonged, and alien enough to make it a perfect escape from the country I felt I had outgrown.

But the city that had once watched a 21-year-old Turkic prince carry his ships over land to drive the Byzantine army from their once-impenetrable fortresses had no interest in my coming-of-age story.

It was busy working through its own shit.

My friend Naveen tells me his mother didn't want him to move to Istanbul, that she was convinced the place was haunted by the violence in its past. It is a Hindu belief that places where blood has been shed can never be at peace. The trauma remains etched into the ancient walls, the soil, the people themselves.

There's a story in the Rāmāyana about a young hermit named Shravan caring for his elderly parents who had lost their sight. Hoping to cure them, he embarks on an epic journey to visit the four most sacred Hindu sites to purify their souls, all while carrying them in baskets attached to the ends of a long bamboo stick that he balanced on his shoulders as he walked.

While travelling through the holy city of Ayodhya, Shravan stopped at a lake to collect water for his parents, but was struck by an arrow launched by the young prince Dasharatha, who mistook him for an elephant. The arrow killed the boy, and when Dasharatha went to seek forgiveness from Shravan's blind parents, they cursed him in anger.

'Just as we are dying due to the separation from our beloved son, you too shall have the same fate.'

Dasharatha would later go on to rule the Kingdom of Kosala and give birth to the deity

Rama, but on his deathbed he remembered the story of Shravan and realised that the curse had ruled his life and found him finally in his death. Hindus believe the curse afflicted not just Dasharatha, but the entire city. Centuries on, thousands would die fighting over it, for honour or greed or religion. Even the lake itself where this fateful death took place, and where a shrine in honour of Shravan now sits, is withering and dying.

Istanbul too has more than its fair share of ghosts looking over its shoulder. Their shadows dance along its banks, drunk on religion and hedonism. The story of stanbul, with its former incarnations as Constantinople and Byzantium, is woven with dizzying glories and plummeting miseries, each pulling at the city's sleeves to keep dancing, a whirling dervish with his hands to the sky, an antenna searching for connection.

Nothing I have seen can match the mascara dust sprinkled along its cheeks at sunset. It takes your breath away when you remember to pay attention to it, and catches you by surprise when you forget. It's no wonder the Turks never want to leave, and when they do they immediately wish to return. My friend Canan cut her trip to Milan short because she missed Istanbul. I didn't get it when she first told me, but I do now.

There is a melancholic magic to the city. Something that pulls you in and doesn't let go.

That brings me back to my theory about Istanbul and the series *Lost*. If you're like me, then you too obsessively consumed this show about a group of strangers who survive a plane crash on a deserted island and have to band together. Of course, the island isn't really deserted, and the crash wasn't really a crash. Over the course of six painfully drawn-out seasons, we learn there is a reason each of the characters was chosen and brought to the island. Each of them is at a crossroad in their lives, forced now to confront their demons in an unforgiving albeit heavenly surrounding, isolated from the world, alone with each other.

Jack was the upstanding citizen and natural leader who was secretly a disgraced surgeon with intense daddy issues. Charlie was the affable and easy-going musician hiding a drug dependency that derailed his ambitions. Jin and Sun were the mistrustful married couple whose backstory was a Shakespearean drama full of crime, betrayal and impossible romance.

They were all thrown together and forced to start anew, a second chance at personal redemption and belonging. At least, until time travel and giant magnets ruined everything.

Maybe I'm just overly romantic, seeing the world through a lens of psychoanalysis, but it really felt like our lives in Istanbul were comparable to *Lost*. Here we were, a group of strangers flung together in a foreign place having to restart our social networks and find our way through cultural and linguistic barriers. Each of us here for a different reason, but all of us seeking a form of escape from what we'd left behind. We were foolish enough to think we'd find it here.

As the blurb for a Netflix drama might put it, the lives of these strangers would soon be unwound by forces hidden beneath the surface of this mysterious paradise. Stress, loneliness and rumours fuelled by boredom and jealousy would lead to fights, emotional and physical. Lifelong friends would be torn apart and pitted against each other. Love stories would end in divorce, several divorces. Some would escape our little island and move on to better things. Most would leave with scars, bitter from betrayal and squandered opportunity. And not all of us would make it out.

From the first day I arrived at the Turkish Radio and Television World offices, work there was intoxicating. An array of wild characters filled our newsroom, shouting at each other over the marching drum of keyboards and fast news. A dozen unique accents could be heard in heated arguments about politics and religion and feminist theory. At lunchtime, hundreds of employees filed in through a prison-style canteen to receive the daily assortment of homemade Turkish food: kuru fasulye, karnıyarık, pilav and a tub of ayran for only three liras. When we grew tired of these meals, we began venturing into nearby centres for burgers or pide. After work, hundreds of staff filed out through the tightly controlled security desk at the entrance, equipped with metal detectors and armed guards, to a row of company shuttles.

Just half a year earlier, the building had been stormed by a rogue military faction that shattered the windows and seized control of the news studio to announce to the world they had overthrown the government, captured the president and shut down all institutions. This wasn't true, but over the course of a few hours on 15 July 2016 the streets of Istanbul were on fire. Two fighter jets bombed the Bosphorus Bridge. Soldiers sprayed the streets with indiscriminate live fire. In response, millions of unarmed citizens had poured out to the streets to defend their democracy, regardless of political conviction. More than 200 would be killed, but the coup was halted in its tracks, making way for an era of sweeping government crackdowns that purged the military, police, state media and universities of all suspected sympathisers.

On the morning of 16 July, my colleagues had returned to the TRT offices to find an armoured tank in the parking lot, abandoned by putschists during their frantic attempts to flee hours earlier.

The most exciting event I had encountered as a journalist up to that point was a standoff in the tiny rural town of Kawerau between four police officers and a drug dealer who later turned himself in.

I found mentorship in Yasmine. She was in many ways the journalist I hoped I'd one day become, and was generous enough to show me guidance amid the madness of our chaotic and mismanaged newsroom. Her eyes would disappear when she smiled, which was often, and in the face of both amusement and awkwardness. One day at work she confronted a colleague clipping his toenails at his desk in the middle of the office, her nervous Kiwi charm disarmed by Turkish pragmatism. We all laughed about it at dinner later—one of the many dinners she organised, crossing paths with strangers and pulling them into her circles.

I looked up to her gallantly and somewhat naively. Oftentimes idolising a person blinds you to their humanity. As you bask in the brilliance of their light, it's easy to miss the cracks forming beneath the surface; hard to recognise the opportunities to pull them back from the edge of their own darkness.

Within a few months of these first surreal introductions, my dear friend and mentor Yasmine died.

It was sudden and incomprehensible. It echoed out to many corners of the world, to people whose lives she had championed and changed, to friends she had touched and inspired in more countries than I have ever visited. To countries like Tunisia and Libya, which she had fought for valiantly through her journalism. To her friends and colleagues in Istanbul, who had admired and gravitated to her fiercely gentle essence.

Those of us who knew her well, who were in her presence in the days and hours before her death, were left with crippling trauma, grief and guilt. Years later, I still clutch at explanations. Maybe a story as linear as a historic curse coursing through a city can explain the collateral damage to the lives of ordinary people.

But of course it is against our nature to pry ourselves from the path of fate. It is difficult to accept that we are not protagonists in a Shakespearean tragedy or a Hindu fable. That we are in fact bystanders passing through the fragile membrane of existence, at times colliding and embracing, transferring heat and light, joy and pain, fear and tranquillity. The noble among us insist on a barter of sincerity, on gifting kindness to the strange bodies floating around us so they too may shine when we burn out.

On a tender Friday two weeks on, with infant winter lapping across the turquoise blanket of the Bosphorus, we held a large memorial service for Yasmine. On the rooftop of a lavish hotel not far from the office, colleagues, friends and family arrived in dark suits and muted dresses, staring in disbelief at each other and making small talk to stay afloat. Children raced in between the white plastic function chairs; hotel catering staff marched in and out with drinks that no one received; the faintest hints of hotel lobby jazz played in the background. At the edge of the terrace, with the enigmatic city folded behind it, stood a large white frame holding Yasmine's image. It was her most recognisable photo, the one she used for her Twitter profile, the one that appeared on articles above her byline. It must have been taken at a conference or a wedding, a fact I deduced from the white-shirted men behind her, engaged in a conversation perhaps she was part of, before the unknown photographer called her name and she swung around, surprised and delighted. The photo captures her head in mid-swing, her blonde waves suspended in the air, framing her glowing cheeks and bashful grin, her eyes squinting artlessly until they hid her pupils. It was the image all of us wanted to remember of Yasmine, radiant and sanguine, abounding with generosity.

I spent the day trying to hold it together, but broke down at the first instance of human contact, weeping into the arms of Hisham and Taha. We found seats somewhere in the middle, and waited for the speeches to begin. Someone asked if I wanted to say something, and I quietly shook my head, sinking further into my seat. I couldn't tell you what was said in that ceremony. It seemed like a damp curtain had fallen, sucking out the sound and the light. How do you even begin to put a lifetime into words? How could any of it make sense?

I washed my face and joined a long line snaking up to the stage, trying not to lose dominion over my limbs. Suddenly I found myself in front of Yasmine's father, Tom, without any words to pull from my pockets. He lifted his arms and wrapped them around me, and when I finally returned his eye contact, he said simply and profoundly:

'Take care of yourself, Mohamed.'

As we slowly gathered into groups to head back to the office in taxis, I saw one of

Yasmine's friends talking to the hotel manager behind the speakers, then taking out her phone and frantically swiping through it. A moment later, the soft jazz ended, and the first jagged falsetto notes of 'Sweet Child o' Mine' burst across the terrace. We stood still, in confusion, before a few of us smiled to ourselves. Guns N' Roses was her favourite band, and this was her favourite song. It was the most appropriate way to end the memorial, a contrast as sudden and disarmingly sweet as our friend. Nothing could have broken the tension quite like the smoky bravado of Slash seducing his Les Paul guitar neck and Axl Rose wailing overhead.

I made my way to the edge of the railing and looked out over the grey apartment towers hugging the crystal water. There must have been an ancient spell that had brought us to this strange and elusive place, that had bound us together with forces we didn't understand. The city gleamed back at me knowingly, refusing to uncup its hands, saying nothing more than it had said to the kings and sultans who tried in vain to dig out its secrets. Instead, the call to prayer suddenly rang out from a mosque below, piercing through the power chords. Then another mosque began, and another, and soon hundreds of minarets were summoning worshippers to make their way inside for Jumaa prayers.

God is great
God is great
I bear witness there is no god but Allah

We watched the scene play out, the muezzins bellowing to the sky, reminding the Istanbulites of the transience of life, the rewards awaiting them on the other side. Howling above, Axl grieved over the memory of a woman he had once known, whose absence left him wandering aimlessly through fog, haunted by the past, asking himself where he should go.

It all made perfect sense, of course, that this would happen here. That I would be standing here to watch it. To be held captive by this moment, this bedevilling, in this city I hated but could never leave. This city whose answers I was not ready to believe. I held my eyes tight and let the noise wash over me, the songs flirting and strangling the air, at times grappling, at times in harmony. They grew louder and messier until all of Istanbul was a canvas of acrylic colours, swirled in circles over and over until it all became one. Until all of us were a single brilliant hue. A muse by which God painted the world.

13

Therapy with Ivanka

THE ONLY TIME I TRULY FELT wealthy was in Turkey. The country was being gripped by its worst economic downturn in decades, but I was young, rich and anxious. It's not that I was paid particularly well—I was still a journalist after all. But because I was an expat, my paycheque arrived in US dollars, while my hardworking Turkish colleagues were trapped in the confines of the spiralling Turkish lira.

When I arrived in 2017, the dollar was worth triple the lira. By 2019, it was worth eight times. This effectively tripled my salary, pushing me into the upper echelons of the country's middle class. I didn't have to worry about my spending, my savings or my rent. For someone who grew up while Auckland's property poverty ballooned into a wasteland, it felt like I was escaping adulthood for a few years. It meant that I could eat out more often, travel and live in the neighbourhood I wanted. It also meant I didn't have to worry about my health, knowing I could get treated at the most extravagant private hospitals in the city. One of these was Liv Hospital, a sprawling shiny complex down the road from our office that featured serviced rooms for overnight patients and fruit-scented drinking water in the lobby. They also had a team of translators who would follow you around and help you speak to the doctors, a godsend for those of us who couldn't quite get our tongues around the complex Turkish grammatical structure, or had the luxury of not having to. Liv Hospital employed hundreds of doctors and had a department for everything from podiatry to plastic surgery. If you showed up with a runny nose, they put you in a comfortable bed for four hours while they ran five blood tests and hooked your arm up to an IV with 'nutrients that will help you feel better'. I never figured out what was in the clear solution they injected me with, but once when I politely turned it down, a nurse looked at me in confusion. 'Are you sure?'

'Yeah, I'll just wait for the test results.'

'Okay. I'll leave it here if you change your mind.'

It only made sense once I came to check out, and watched the receptionist print out an exhaustive list of services to charge my insurance company with.

    Blood pressure check
    General health check
    Blood test for hepatitis C
    Blood test for HIV

Nutrient solution IV drip
Prescription for paracetamol
Total cost: 1350 Turkish lira

 It was a stretch from the government-subsidised community clinics my grandmother would take us to in Giza, where doctors would tour around, spending three hours at each branch trying to get through as many patients as possible before they disappeared for another week. We'd sit on plastic benches in a roofless lobby with forty other people ailing from ear infections, diabetes and high cholesterol. It was a day-long ordeal, like everything in Egypt is. In New Zealand we were treated like human beings and had access to world-class facilities, but ACC claims were clunky and unreliable, and wait times for specialists were months long. If you lived in a poorer suburb, you got cheaper GP visits but worse facilities, and if you lived in a better-equipped area, you paid sixty dollars just to get a prescription signed.

 In Turkey, I could get sick without worrying about access to great healthcare or how to pay for it. This must be what the rich feel like all the time. Some of my expat friends brought forward upcoming surgeries so they didn't have to fork out for crippling bills back home, or made use of the city's iconic hair implant industry that promised tourists a hotel stay and tour of the city as part of the package. In Taksim there's always a gaggle of men with compression bandages around their heads eating baklava and simit in between implant sessions. Enjoy the Ottoman hospitality. Meet like-minded middle-aged men. Go home with a lush head of hair. What's not to like?

After Yasmine's death, I found myself navigating a more expensive segment of Turkey's health industrial complex. I avoided it at first, stubbornly pushing through the days while my body tried to deal with grief by turning against itself.

But maintaining my denial was impossible. In the days that followed, I was asked to retell the events of the night Yasmine died to dozens of people—managers, friends, strangers, journalists, family members, police and a number of people who'd found my number or social media accounts and sent through frantic questions of genuine concern. In quiet hours I was left replaying each vivid detail in my head. Moments would emerge in my dreams, or appear suddenly during a conversation or at home. It felt visceral, like I was being transported back in time. Like a dog emerging from water, my body would begin to shake involuntarily, and I would become fearful of everything around me.

Eventually the panic attacks synced with my broken circadian rhythm and scheduled an episode at the same time each day. On the bus coming into the office each morning, I would feel a low hum building, a chorus of foreboding whispers that got louder and louder until, with a crescendo, they drowned everything else out. They chanted in unison like Macbeth's witches, warning me that something terrible was coming.

By midday it would be at its full height. I'd have to leave my desk and wander out to the edge of the lawn outside the office, overlooking the Bosphorus. I'd sit on the grass and try to focus on the cargo ships passing under the newly renamed 15 July Martyrs Bridge, trying to ignore my quickening breath, the tightness crawling across my chest. Once while walking through a sprawling shopping centre I became overwhelmed by the number of people around, the noise, the noise. I couldn't find where the exit was. Every direction stretched impossibly. I locked myself in a bathroom cubicle and tried to slow my breathing down. I focused on the white walls around me. It seemed to calm things down. When I emerged to find my mother and sister, who'd come to visit me a few days earlier, they both looked at me in shock. I was completely drained.

The media company I worked for offered to send me to their occupational therapist, who was not ready to deal with my situation. She stared wide-eyed at me as I told her the story, and through her limited English searched for words of comfort. Tears began to well in the corner of her eyes. Surely therapists weren't supposed to cry?

'What if you think of it all like a TV show?'

'What do you mean?'

'Like a Turkish drama, you know? And you're just someone sitting behind a TV watching it all from the safety of your couch. Then it won't be so bad.'

Coming here was a mistake.

A week later, my friend Canan suggested a private clinic, and I agreed. The office was in a swanky part of Nişantaşı, opposite a hotel and a five-star restaurant. The receptionist asked me to take my shoes off and slip shower caps over my feet before I went in. I sat in the '80s art deco lobby surrounded by burnt-beige chairs and dim bedroom lamps until the therapist was ready. His office was somehow even darker, illuminated by an intense orange desk lamp, and he sat in a turtleneck and gelled-back hair, listening to me with the hint of a smirk at the corner of his mouth.

'That is very interesting, your story.'

'I guess.'

He motioned for me to continue, the gleam in his eyes sharpening. A half-filled ashtray sat on the desk, interrogated by the spotlight from the lamp. Next to it was a silver flip lighter, a pile of paperback novels, and a crystal whiskey glass. He wasn't wearing shower cap shoes.

'Here in my practice, I like to assign my clients homework. But don't get worried, this is not like school homework.'

'Okay.'

'Each week I will give you a book to read, and the next week we can discuss what you thought about it.'

'...'

'For the first week, I want you to read *The Alchemist*. I think you will find it very helpful.'

I paid the 400 TL at the lobby and told the receptionist I didn't want to book a follow-up session. I didn't want to talk to anyone.

The next day I returned to the office, although I'd been sternly told to take some time off and get some rest. As I made my way past the body scanner and the final turnstile into reception, I looked up to see a 'breaking news' ticker flash at the bottom of the large LED screen behind Pervin, the receptionist. 'HAMAS DECLARES THIRD INTIFADA.'

My eyes lit up. My spidey senses tingled. Donald Trump had just announced he was moving the US embassy from Tel Aviv to Jerusalem, declaring the holy city as the 'undivided capital of Israel', stirring the 2000-year-old bones of an Abrahamic territorial battle and rousing the fury of Palestinians, who were being slowly and methodically pushed out of the Old City and its surrounding suburbs to make way for Israeli settlers. The devastating Second Intifada was ignited after Israeli leader Ariel Sharon had paraded through Al Aqsa Mosque with an entourage of politicians and soldiers. Seventeen years later, surrounded by Christmas baubles, Trump stood behind a White House podium and read a carefully prepared statement explaining why he was kicking a hornets' nest while wearing the flower dress from the end of *Midsommar*.

'I've judged this course of action to be in the best interests of the United States of America, and the pursuit of peace between Israel and the Palestinians.'

Off screen, gazing up at him in blissful admiration, stood his daughter, Ivanka Trump, and her husband, Jared Kushner. Five months later they would be in Jerusalem unveiling the plaque at the shiny new embassy, while protesters in Gaza were being shot by Israeli snipers.

I watched the Hamas leader calling for a Palestinian uprising on the screen in reception, then stormed downstairs and straight into my manager's office.

'Welcome back, Mohamed. How are you feeling?'

'You need to send me to Jerusalem.'

'What? Are you sure you're ready?'

'Yes. I can leave this afternoon.'

The next week I spent running from tear gas and police horses, documenting the anger and frustration of Palestinians. Israeli soldiers fired stun grenades into crowds of families, ripped Palestinian flags from the hands of teenagers and dragged women by their hijabs. My editor warned me to stay behind the soldiers or they would shoot at me, and of course I didn't listen. Whenever an explosion went off, I gravitated towards it. I held my iPhone in front of my face and livestreamed everything I saw. The adrenaline drowned out everything else. It was a peculiar calm, to be surrounded by as much chaos outside as there was inside me. If anxiety followed the law of osmosis, then here, for a few days, my internal and external worlds were in equilibrium.

My colleague Hossam came back to Istanbul with a scar on his arm from the shrapnel of a stun grenade. I came back with a rubber-coated steel bullet that one soldier had fired at me to stop me from filming a protest in Bethlehem. It rocketed into the back of my press vest and almost knocked me off my feet. We collected them as souvenirs, taking the lead from Palestinians who turned irony into an act of resistance. In the tiny neighbourhood of Nabi Saleh, they protested each Friday to stop an illegal settlement encroaching on their land. Israeli forces responded by firing hundreds of tear gas canisters into their streets and homes. On Saturday, the women in the village collect the empty canisters and hang them up in their front yards, planting flowers and tomatoes in the stun grenades. Every house is lined with them, a living exhibit of radical persistence. Their anger made sense, the forces threatening their world wore helmets and drove armoured vehicles. I was returning to the privilege of safety and the security of a Western passport. What did I have to be stressed about?

    Back in Istanbul, I attempted to burrow back into my old life and shrug off the nagging omens, but it was no use. Days began to slow and decay. I paced around my flat waiting for an Amazon delivery that never arrived, waiting for sleep that always had the wrong directions. A high-pitched string orchestra played underneath my social interactions, public transportation and grocery shopping. I was stuck.

A week later, a friend sent me the address of a specialist deep into the Asian side of the Bosphorus, and I found myself standing in front of a looming hospital building that had drawn architectural inspiration from a Marvel Supervillain.

NPST ANBUL BRAIN HOSPITAL.

I thought about DiCaprio in *Shutter Island*, showing up to investigate the mental institute he was already a patient in. Like him, I had been distracting myself with other people's conspiracies to avoid confronting my own. Was it better to live as a monster, or die as a good man?

Through the clear glass revolving doors, under a ceiling fan blasting hot air in the faces of unwitting pedestrians, I signed myself up for a mental health assessment and a translator. Three storeys up from the reception, I was seated in a small white room while a rugby helmet adorned with red and blue wires was placed over my head.

'You will see some flashing lights in front of your eyes. Please look away from them.'

I waited for Beethoven's Ninth to play, but thankfully it didn't. Instead, I watched faint white dots appear and disappear at the corners of my eyes and tried not to stare at them. The heating was up just a little too high. The faint murmur of angry Istanbul traffic hugged the walls, filling the otherwise awkward silence between my chair and the nurse, who sat on a dusty computer from the mid-2000s, squinting at waves of blue light passing through my cerebral cortex. On the screen, the squiggly parts of my brain lit up in yellow and green. My neurons were waking up and shaking hands, trading jokes in an ancient language that held the secrets to my disorder.

'Everything looks okay here, but you seem stressed.'

Two floors higher, blood samples were taken and analysed for a hundred known diseases. I sipped burnt coffee at the cafeteria while medical professionals sucked cigarettes and gossiped about their patients. I flicked a gold coin into the side of a massage chair and closed my eyes, waiting for calm to set in. Two hours later, an impossibly put-together woman approached me, wearing a silk black turtleneck and matching eyeliner.

'You are Mohamed?'

'Yes.'

'I am your translator.'

A tall and striking Iraqi woman, married to a Turkish businessman and working part-time at the hospital mostly for something to do, she became my companion each time I visited the hospital, sitting in on medical consultations to explain what was happening, and translating my answers from broken Arabic to broken Turkish. In this way, she came to know almost everything about my life and health, mental and physical. In the hours we spent during each visit waiting for the sluggish bureaucracy of this mammoth private hospital, I would hang out with her at the café and listen to stories about Turkish housewives and compound life.

Her name wasn't Ivanka, but I began referring to her that way to friends until I forgot her actual name. She'd had surgical procedures to lift her cheekbones and streamline her nose, and that—combined with her dyed blonde hair and slender build—made her look almost exactly like the US First Daughter. The resemblance was so uncanny that I saved her number on my phone as 'Ivanka Hospital', obviously to differentiate her from the other Ivankas I knew. Each time I'd reach reception ahead of my appointments, I'd panic when asked which translator I was after. I contemplated once showing them a photo of the Trump heiress from a Google search. Once during a medical exam, I absent-mindedly asked where 'Ivanka' had gone, and was met with blank stares. Maybe one of the doctors connected those dots later, or maybe they just thought I was hallucinating.

It made a strange sort of sense that Ivanka would pop into my life now, like a well-placed referential joke at the heart of a Sorkin screenplay. After my initial brain scan and health checks, I made an appointment with one of the psychologists for later that week, and bid Ivanka farewell.

'Make sure you call me when you come back for your appointment.'

I waited for a taxi outside the front doors of the hospital in a state of delirium. I had officially become a crazy person, standing outside a hospital for crazy people. I put on my headphones and jumped around in a puddle left behind by morning rain while Kanye rapped about his love for Kanye. People stared, but could they really judge a man walking out of a brain hospital? Of course not.

Each time I went to the hospital, I'd spend hours catching the lift from one floor to the other, meeting a psychiatrist at 10am, then waiting to meet the psychologist at 2pm, then chilling at the café for another hour before my bill was processed and I could pay the exorbitant amount and find a taxi back to the office. In the downtime, I would wander through the hallways looking for Ivanka, who'd jump at the opportunity to pass the time with one of the few Arabic-speaking patients at the hospital. She was easy to spot, waltzing around the café in a Burberry trench coat one day, a purple satin blouse the next, her hair professionally blow-dried.

'None of the Turkish women in my compound really like me. I miss my friends in Dubai.'

'That doctor is a real asshole, but she doesn't know that we all know about her divorce.'

'You must come over one night for dinner with me and my husband.'

On my second visit, I met a soft-spoken psychologist named Elif. She'd studied at Harvard, spoke English in an Americanised Turkish accent, and watched me quietly as I walked through the door and awkwardly took the seat in front of her. She sat calmly and waited for me to begin speaking, content to let silence swirl around our chairs and fill the room. Her eyes seemed far away, like she was watching herself talking to me through a two-way mirror. I felt the bees begin to stir from their nest and zigzag around my throat.

'Sorry, do you mind if I use the bathroom?'

'Of course, go ahead.'

I fast-walked out into the hallway, where Ivanka was falling asleep on the couch. In the bathroom mirror, I threw water on my face and watched my hands slowly unclench over the sink. Ten minutes later I waddled back into the leather seat, smiling in the way I do when I feel uncomfortable.

'Is this your way of avoiding bringing up what happened?'

'N-no ... not at all.'

Elif wasn't messing around. I straightened my back and stared at my shoes. 'I've just told this story so many times, it's starting to feel like a speech.'

'I understand.'

'I'm just exhausted, you know?'

'That seems like an appropriate response.'

Elif stared at the fluffy maroon of the carpet as I slowly began to unfurl. I searched her face for intrigue but came up empty. Instead, I watched her trace an invisible circle on her work pad like she was practising for a game show or conjuring a protective spell. When I went quiet, she tilted her eyes up and frowned.

'Why are you surprised that you're feeling anxious?'

'Heh ... yeah.'

'I want you to think of yourself as having an energy vial, like in a video game. That night, you used up your entire energy bar just to get through it. And now you have no strength left. It's all gone, and it'll take some time to refill again. Be patient, and be kind to yourself in the meantime.'

Once the hour was up, she let me walk out without issuing me homework or even asking for a follow-up appointment. I walked to the nurse at reception and found the earliest booking. A layer of rust had been sandpapered off my skin and I felt raw. It was the first authentic feeling that had showed up in a while.

When the taxi pulled over at the gates of TRT, its staggering corporate nationalism seemed a little tamer. I scanned my card through the turnstile and shuffled in, turning it around so I could see myself beaming up from the plastic, alive and limitless. Six months younger, but a world away. In the glassy black reception tiles I found another version of myself staring back. Red lightning around my cornea. A haunting in my cheeks. Both were strangers, travellers from competing timelines that didn't belong here. Or maybe I was the alien, a naive and dreamy-eyed expat coming to grips with the cold reality beyond the walls of home.

At my desk I found a small package waiting for me. My friend Asmaa had just returned from a trip to the southern Turkish city of Konya, a deeply spiritual city with delicate white mosques steeped in snow for at least four months of every year. At its heart is a burial chamber where the thirteenth-century Persian poet Rumi rests. My Sufi friends visited him every year to attend a four-day celebration marking his birthday.

The lululemon hipsters may tell you Rumi wrote beautiful and timeless love poems, but almost all his work is about God. His jubilant sonnets and aching laments weren't intended to be divorced from their Islamic context. Instead, they show the softness in the religion lost to the anger of today's world.

Inside the small package was a gift: an anthology of Rumi's most iconic poetic works. There was no message accompanying the book; it was just a small but determined gesture.

I sat down and flipped the vibrant cover open to the first poem, titled 'The Guest House', and time ground to a halt.

> This being human is a guest house
> Every morning a new arrival
> A joy, a depression, a meanness
> Some momentary awareness comes
> As an unexpected visitor

As a poet I am aware of the sorcery of words. A man once told me one of my poems brought back the pain of losing his best friend to cancer, an experience I knew nothing about, and had not intended to convey. But sometimes intentions aren't irrelevant, and words worm their way through the cosmos to find you.

> Even if they're a crowd of sorrows
> Who violently sweep your house

> Empty of its furniture
> Still, treat each guest honourably

I had been fighting against grief, refusing to sit and converse with this visitor that had barged through my living-room door waving their arms wildly in the air. I didn't know what they wanted, but I'd never given them the time to speak. We are trained to expel foreign presences from our bodies, warring to cleanse ourselves from change, even if it comes as medicine.

> The dark thought, the shame, the malice
> Meet them at the door laughing
> And invite them in

A few days later, I received a call from Ivanka, letting me know that Elif had returned to the United States with her husband, and I needed to be transferred to another therapist. She asked when I'd be available for a new appointment, and I told her I would let her know. I'm sure she told me her name when I picked up the phone, but for the life of me I can't remember it. On the screen above my work desk, the real Ivanka was giving an interview on ABC News. She defended her father's policies, his views on women, and the children held in detention centres at the border. As a mother, she said it was heart-breaking to see children locked up, but it was the president's job 'to protect our country's security'.

I decided to skip the work shuttle and walk home, through the sweaty dust of Istanbul's rush hour. The warring horns and car bonnets edging their sunburnt lips into every empty space reminded me of my childhood in Cairo. It was something about the endless noise of twenty million jazz musicians soloing to the steady drumbeat of city life. There was a logic to it, a wayward beauty that never let you forget you were smaller and more insignificant than you thought. That around you a machinery churned and screamed and you were a tiny cog who had life to live, too. If you opened yourself to it, let the chaos seep into your bones and tango with your intestines, then soon you realised it wasn't here to stay. An uncouth tourist parading through your underwear drawer, or a panic attack barrelling down your windpipe, it wasn't here to stay. You could fight, every day, to keep your tiny world in order, or you could turn up the music and teach yourself how to dance.

14

The peace of wild things

MUSLIM CHILDREN ARE USUALLY TAUGHT HOW to pray from the age of around seven. By that point, they've spent years curiously watching and imitating their parents and older siblings when they kneel over in unison and touch their foreheads and noses to the ground. As infants, they often find the sudden lack of attention from the adults in their life provocative and try to interrupt it, or think it a game in which they can participate by climbing on to the back of their father as he prostrates, or hiding inside the folds of their mother's long prayer garments. Once, while deep in group prayer with my father and brother Sherif, my one-year-old nephew paraded into the living room, and contorted his tiny body to squeeze between our legs like bars on a jungle gym. All this while singing along to his favourite YouTube song of the week: 'Baby Shark'.

With the least self-control in the group, I buckled first. A smirk snuck in from the inside of my stomach and wiggled to the corner of my face. I shook it off and tried with all my might to focus on my Quran recitation, but it was no use. Like a shark smelling blood, Zayn focused his attention on me, realising he had found his audience. He waddled his little feet across our prayer mats and stood in front of me trying to catch my gaze. When it came time to bend our backs into a kneeling position, Zayn mimicked it without breaking his stare, looking up at me through his legs, his chubby hands planted on the ground in front of him for support. I tried to cough to cover up a chuckle, but that only emboldened him. He started edging backwards towards me, still with his hands planted and his upside-down grin knowing and daring. When I slipped and my eyes caught his, it was all over. I erupted in a hysterical fit of laughter, which travelled to my brother through our connected shoulders. He started laughing too. Zayn was overjoyed at his master plan falling into place.

We had to start our prayers all over again.

By the time a young Muslim reaches puberty, they are expected to perform the ritual of prayer five times a day. The first is fajr, prayed just before the break of dawn. Then is thuhr, prayed at high noon. Then asr, the afternoon prayer. At sunset, Maghrib. And finally, isha, prayed just after twilight. The supplications follow the path of the sun each day, and their timings differ in each part of the world, stretching and shrinking throughout the year. In the middle of winter, fajr can be prayed as late as 7am in New Zealand, but in summer it gets as early as 3am. In countries close to the Arctic, where the sun barely sets for six months of the year, Muslims have to figure out how to adjust their prayer times in a way that makes sense. What unites each one of the nearly two billion faithful worldwide is that our direction of prayer has a singular focal point. When we lay out our prayer mats and begin to converse with the Lord, we do it facing the Kaaba, the iconic black cubic structure at the heart of Mecca. Since the time of Prophet Muhammad (peace be upon him), Muslims have been directing themselves towards Mecca. When I was lucky enough to visit in 2013 during my pilgrimage, I watched as millions of human beings from every inch of the globe arranged themselves in hundreds of concentric circles around the Kaaba, stood shoulder to shoulder, and raised their hands to the sky. During the Hajj rituals, I orbited with my fellow believers around the enigmatic monument, wrapped in nothing but white robes that made me indistinguishable from the sea of worshippers around me. In this moment we were truly equal. No one could tell who was rich and who was poor, who belonged to a high-ranking family and who was an orphan. We prayed together, slept alongside each other and poured our hearts out, hoping to return cleansed of our past and closer to our inner selves.

My father told me that a Muslim can go through many spiritual phases in his life. He will have doubts and stare at the stars in anguish at times, but he should never let go of his prayer. It is the link that persists with God that never closes, and as long as a person reopens that channel five times a day, then ultimately he'll be alright.

When my friend Yasmine died a few years after my pilgrimage, a looming terror gripped me. I found myself afraid of the world, fixated on real and imagined threats that hid in the shadows and intended harm to loved ones I was unable to protect. If someone in my family fell ill, I worried about losing them forever. If they left somewhere on a plane, I obsessively checked the departure and arrival times in case of a crash.

It was the first time I had struggled with anxiety, and it entered my life with the subtlety of a steam engine breaking through the living-room wall. Sometimes I couldn't tell where the anxiety faded and my natural paranoia began. At times, they tag-teamed to invent ways to keep me up at night.

I had many friends who'd suffered from debilitating anxiety disorders. I'd had my fair share of late nights trying to steady someone over the phone while they had a full-blown panic attack in a supermarket, or held someone until their breathing returned slowly. Sometimes, telling jokes helped quiet the storm; other times, physical touch. I thought of myself as a calming presence others could anchor their chaos to, that I had enough grounding to keep their nervous kites from flying away. That is, until it was my time to face the dragon.

It always started with a small and sincere thought, a bothering, a word a loved one or colleague tossed carelessly into my lap before departing. That's all it took, a whiff of blood, and the beast roared with hunger. The tiny thought would then grow and spin and quake until it engulfed everything around me. Sometimes forcing myself to sleep, or throwing headphones on and playing music I knew the lyrics to, helped. Sometimes it only served as a soundtrack to the cheap sci-fi horror I was trapped in, forced to survive alongside a screaming bespectacled kid and a sweaty mayor who had to unite the town or face extinction.

It wasn't until the next morning that I'd be able to assess the wreckage, send a civil defence crew to rescue the elderly from their homes. It was never as bad as it looked, but in the throes of an anxiety attack, I lost all sense of grounding.

I tried medicating myself into numbness—taking the edge off, as the tobacco enthusiasts say. A doctor in Turkey prescribed me a heavy dose of Xanax, a drug you can't get your hands on back home. It felt like it could be the answer. If Chance the Rapper and Mac Miller thought it was cool enough to rap about, then maybe it'd prove to be a good time. Instead, Xanax dimmed things to the point I was barely able to get out of bed, catch the bus to work or hold conversations with anyone. It gave me tunnel vision, blurring the edges of my day so they bled into the focal points. How did people do this at parties?

A few people asked if they could buy a few tabs off me for their Saturday nights, and I resisted handing a Molotov cocktail to anarchists. A few months later, Mac Miller died from an overdose after years of battling with an addiction to Lean, a toxic combination of cough syrup and soda that's often combined with Xanax tablets.

I abandoned the pharmaceutical route and looked for something more 'natural'. Despite harsh legal penalties, weed was pretty easy to get in Istanbul. Some of it was grown locally in rural farms or people's apartments. Most of it was smuggled in from Scandinavian countries, and I was told it was the 'good stuff'. I had tried it a few times in the past to mixed results, but I'd never actually bought it myself. I met up with an affable Turkish guy outside the downtown compound he and his girlfriend lived in, and he gave me my first three grams. He then invited me to come up and join a party he and his friends were throwing, and I politely declined.

'No problem, man. Hey, let's hang out sometime. You seem like a cool dude.'

Unfortunately I never had the pleasure.

It made total sense from a logical standpoint. I was struggling with anxiety. Weed was a downer that was supposed to mellow you out. Makes sense, right? I'd spent enough time around stoners in high school to know they always seemed more chill and careless while high, and that's exactly the space I needed to be in. For a while, it did the job. On days when my body felt overwhelmed by stress, when the shadows churned up my throat and squeezed, I smoked up. It had a similar effect to Xanax, but much milder. It also allowed me to focus on simple things and not get lost in my own subconscious. I binged a lot of terrible TV during this period, got hooked on shows like *Insatiable* and *Brooklyn Nine-Nine* that demanded nothing from me mentally or emotionally. It was just what I needed, a switch for my prefrontal cortex that had begun creaking and wheezing from the pressure. It was good until it wasn't.

Soon I realised my self-medication was beginning to falter. Instead of focusing on whatever whimsical law enforcement shenanigan Andy Samberg was up to, I began to focus on the little thoughts squirming behind my eyes. Then the real paranoia kicked in, and boy was that a ride. From a dark cave at the bottom of a forgotten dungeon in Mordor, the dragon raised its head and smiled. It had found a way in—I had handed it the keys. High and unguarded, without the full grasp of my deductive reasoning, I became the perfect victim for its mischief.

I retained enough sense to be aware of how little control I had over this carnival of paranoia cackling into an unkept night. I'd show up to work the next day physically exhausted, unable to work or interact with friends. I was churning myself into the ground, and I didn't know what to do.

When the fasting month of Ramadan began, I saw it as an opportunity to try to put things on hold. Alongside the food and water I was abstaining from as part of my Islamic practice from sunrise to sunset each day, I decided I would stop smoking for the entire month. Muslims were encouraged to perform extra prayers and read the Quran regularly throughout the month, and reflect on their relationship with Allah. Through hunger, worship and reflection, the purpose was to embrace your vulnerability before God and purify your heart. But in order to clear my heart, I needed to clear my head.

The first few days were a challenge. One of the side effects to marijuana withdrawal that your high school friends don't tell you about is restlessness. You feel bored all the damn time, become aware of the mundanity of the world around you. But the daily practices kept my mind busy. I woke up at 2.30 to have yoghurt and fruit before the dawn prayer marking the start of my fast. After each salat during the day, I read a small section of the Quran. In the evening, I'd spend an hour preparing my meal, and break my fast on three dates and a coffee (the coffee withdrawals hit me much harder than anything else), before praying the dusk prayer. After I'd finished dinner and watched an episode of something on Netflix, I would get up and pray the nightly taraweeh prayers, reading larger sections of the Quran between each prostration. The aim was to finish a chapter each night, so by the time the month drew to a close with the birth of the new moon, I would have completed all thirty chapters of the Quran. Only the fast is a requirement in Islamic teachings, but the recitations and the extra prayers are encouraged, and are often much easier to accomplish in Ramadan than at any other time during the year.

We're told this is because the worst of the devils are chained up during this month, and whether that's a metaphor for our own tamed egos or not, it does feel like something within the body softens while fasting.

There is a concept in particular called *khushuah* that describes the state of concentration and presence one should aspire towards during the ritual of prayer. In this state, one shrugs off the pestering demands of the real world and focuses only on the acts of worship and the passages of the Quran read during each prayer. It becomes a portal through which a worshipper enters and isolates themselves from worldly distractions. I want to stress the aspirational nature of this concept—in reality, few people are able to achieve this. When you're a kid, all you think about while praying is everything else you're not doing right now—video games, cartoons, what your friends are up to. At the back of the mosque, me and my friends desperately tried to concentrate during group prayers, but ultimately the joker in the group with some form of attention deficit disorder would try to make us laugh. We always did end up laughing, and received stern looks from our dads, who in turn received disapproving looks from the older uncles in the mosque.

As an adult, life becomes even more distracting, and in prayer your thoughts quickly dart towards work, relationship issues and food. It's a lifelong struggle to bring about the kind of focus and concentration needed to reap the benefits of prayer. In the times that I've allowed myself the openness and vulnerability to really commit myself, I found a secret space I could slip into and let my mind and heart heal. There was a sweetness in the vacuum left after pushing out all other thoughts, a material silence that covered your bones and held you. It felt safe here, and I longed to remain in its tranquillity. During Hajj, ten days into a pilgrimage with nothing to do but pray and recite and reflect, I began to taste this sweetness, the joy of cleansing the toxins from my limbs. When I returned to my dusty material life, Sherif noticed a glow around me. I felt it, too—an aura that held me by my shoulders and gently lifted me up. I also felt it slowly fading, day by day, as I slipped inevitably back into my old routines and the trivialities of life.

My brother would soon be gifted another type of *khushuah,* the birth of his two sons, Zayn and Zak. From the moment they entered our world, they demanded everything, and I watched Sherif transform into a person who could fulfil their needs. There was a glow about him that tamed his wild. It emanated kindness and calm towards everyone, but especially towards his children, who orbited him in complete devotion. I watch him rolling on the carpet with an ecstatic Zak raised high above his head. Meanwhile, Zayn races around the kitchen in his plastic push-car, but takes a turn too sharply and loses balance, hitting his head on the floor and erupting into screams. He runs straight past our worried arms into the living room and buries his entire body into his father's chest. I swear, the light emanating from my brother's eyes at this moment could power all of Auckland.

When I looked after them, I began to understand a little of what parenthood asks of you. Even after just an hour of chasing the two boys around the house to make sure they were always in my sight, trying to keep them entertained and their hyperactive curiosity satisfied, I found myself physically spent. Being around them offered a joy I had not felt anywhere else before, a completeness. Their gift was in making you feel like a galaxy, expansive and illuminated. In turn you gave them all of your presence, holding on to them with both of your hands so that that moment never slipped. Only in reflection later do you realise that this is why you feel so tired, and so in love. Zayn and Zak had achieved what no drug or therapist could do; they reminded me to detach myself from the past and to stop fearing the future. All their emotions were expressed fully: happiness and pain wholly committed to in the moment they existed, and forgotten completely in the next. I had to match their energy if I wanted to keep up, and I could only do that if I let everything else go.

This was what my Sunday-school Islamic teachers had tried to tell us about prayer, about what God demanded of us in the moments we put down our toys and turn to him. Bring nothing with you, not your past or your present, just yourself and an open heart.

It is also what my body demanded of me. To let go of all the things I couldn't change, the people I couldn't save, the past that wanted to live on but had no business in doing so. To let go of all of the parallel timelines that branched like lightning strikes into the fog, a million terrifying possibilities that only existed in my mind. I had to unclench my fists and watch them all slip through my fingertips, wash my hands and feet the way I was taught when I was a child longing for nothing but the present. Sit in the stillness of now and let it hold me. Sink my fingertips into the carpet and feel the ground pressing its gentle weight against me, the air wash up on my skin, my lungs balloon and sigh. I am going to be okay.

    Bismillah.

15

Still life with a pool of dreams

TO'ASAVILI WAS DREAMING OF COWS SWIMMING under the sea.

Andy ruined a cosplay event by spilling his drink on the PA system.

During the first lockdown, buckled into my parents' house watching the world begin to end, I began having the strangest dreams. They came crashing into my life. Vivid. Anxious. Surreal. Every night, without fail, I was plunged into a parallel universe in which I was burdened by a weighted sense of importance and tasked with playing a vital role in a mystery of my own making.

One night, I was bartending a jazz event in Washington DC hosted by Jon Stewart (yes, *the* Jon Stewart) before abandoning my post halfway so I could register to vote in the midterm elections. Except all the polling booths were closed and I had no money for the bus.

Another night I found a pair of AirPods that let me see the last memory of their owner, which happened to be the final moments of a sailing apprenticeship training programme that had ended in a deadly shipping accident. Now I had to investigate to free the young sailing student who'd been framed for it.

It was too much pressure.

I was curious about why I was suddenly having this uninterrupted string of fantastical dreams, why they all felt so real, and why they were all so damn stressful. I posted something about it on social media, only to be met with a flood of similar stories from my friends all over the world. It turned out, I wasn't alone.

Tali was accepted into a haven for lucid dreamers.

Kirsti uncovered Nick Cave's darkest secret (turns out he's a cannibal).

Amy got a massive crest tattoo across her stomach that said '100% British' (she's not British).

This was happening all over the world, all at the same time. I received stories from people in different countries, different time zones and different walks of life. They were all just as perplexed as to why these inexplicable dreams were visiting them each night.

It became a strand that connected us—intrepid sleepers journeying into the abyss, fighting angry cosplayers, Australian rock stars and the collective anxiety that we all felt, that was overwhelming us all. In response we conjured highly stressful but utterly nonsensical dreams.

In California, Briana's indoor waterfall feature flooded her house.

In Istanbul, Laurelie brought a squid back to life in a flowerpot.

In London, Mahmoud practised his spells for a war against other parts of the United Kingdom. (Also, he was Harry Potter.)

What was the meaning of all this?

Well, I wasn't the only one collecting dreams. Several research institutions worldwide have been conducting studies on the phenomenon, collecting data and stories, attempting to decipher what it means and what it says about our brains. The Lyon Neuroscience Research Center found that after France went into its first mandated lockdown, people began having dreams that were 35 per cent more vivid. A 2015 study by the Turku Brain and Mind Center in Finland found that anxiety can often lead to a lot of bad dreams.

There also does seem to be a link between irregular sleeping patterns and weird dreams. We tend to have most of our dreams during the deeper REM stage of our sleep cycles. So if, like me, you ended up staying up into the spooky hours of the morning and sleeping in more often, your chances of having vivid dreams were much higher because our brains were forcing us into longer REM periods of sleep to make up for the change in our circadian rhythms.

Studies done in the past have also shown links between traumatic events and dreams on a societal scale. After the September 11 attacks, people across the United States began to have disturbing and vivid dreams, processing their trepidation at night when everything finally went quiet.

It's no wonder, then, that in the throes of the historically uncertain times we had found ourselves in, we were turning to our subconscious for answers. Dipping our mind's toe into the murky waters of the sleep world in search of comfort or meaning, but instead finding suppressed and confused emotions lurking beneath the surface. We yearned to escape into the cosmos and feed our need for adventure, connection, and purpose, but instead found ourselves trapped at home.

And so, locked up, our minds wandered.

16

A pirate's life

I

LIVING IN LONDON IN THE SECOND season of the global pandemic, I got back into video games in a huge way. For years, I hadn't used my PS4 for anything except watching Netflix. I had abandoned my gaming past once I realised I could fit more writing and performing into every square inch of my life if I did. But my friends Naveen and Mustafa were big on it, and when we found ourselves locked down in three separate elbows of the world, they talked me into buying an Xbox so we could all play together. Soon it became a ritual, calling each other up after work for an hour or two (or four) of first-person shooter action. Nav was a natural, having persistently played during his teenage years, and Mustafa was a quick learner. I wasn't, often struggling to aim and not get killed at the beginning of every round by the hordes of faceless online players from across Europe and the Asia-Pacific. Me and Nav would log on at night, and Mustafa would join us from Sydney as soon as he woke up. We'd watch him on a

FaceTime screen as he ground his specialty coffee beans and crafted a latte that would make a Surry Hills barista blush. We'd exchange dumb jokes well below our age expectations and gently tease each other, before updating the others on our latest pursuits and side hustles.

Nav had just released the latest edition of his NFT project (if you don't know what NFTs are I'm the wrong person to explain them to you), a sprawling digital comic series set a hundred years in the future. Mustafa, a journalist, was chasing down leads on a story about a Lebanese community leader taking on the Catholic Church's monopoly over gravesites in Sydney. I was working on this book and trying not to let the videos coming out of Gaza overwhelm me.

The constant connection with my friends helped me navigate the loneliness of a strange city, which had been compounded by the isolation of Covid restrictions. It also helped me manage my usual latent anxiety, which loved to lurk in the shadows and peacock around the edges of my living room when the sun went down, which in the London winter was at 4pm. Our nightly phone calls became a distraction I desperately latched on to—they got me through to bed before I had time to think unsupervised.

Whenever a new game popped up on our radars, we'd all download it and wander into its world together. *Splitgate* was an immediate favourite, an arcade-style shoot 'em up where you could set up portals anywhere on the map and teleport yourself instantly. Once I got the hang of it, I learnt how to teleport myself behind an enemy as he chased me, to take him out successfully using the element of surprise. *Outriders* was more challenging, an epic sci-fi story set on an alien planet with dark secrets. We were the soldiers granted strange magical powers and tasked with exploring the unrelenting wilderness, fighting monsters and wayward humans who'd defected from home base. It sounded great on paper, but the game went out of its way to make progression nearly impossible, sending waves of relentless enemies at you and your crew and leaving you little room for escape. I found myself getting frustrated when I failed to complete a mission; the game seemed designed to force you into numerous tries until you learnt the patterns and strategies of the AI. I would turn the console off each night and feel the blood coursing through my body. Not what I needed, thanks.

One day, Mustafa shared a video for a niche game that had been released a few years earlier but hadn't gathered enough momentum to compete with the big titles. It was a pirate-themed adventure game called *Sea of Thieves*, where groups of players formed crews of two to four and were gifted a ship, usually a sloop or a brigantine, and left to wander the expanse of the open sea filled with dozens of other online sailors. There were hundreds of islands to explore, each with hidden booty and undead spirits in the thick jungle, awaiting foolhardy pirates with bloodlust and a thirst for glory. As you can tell, we took to the game like scurvy to a poop deck. With FaceTime open on our phones and split between our dimly lit faces, we coordinated our voyage through a series of commands and giddy exclamations, often yelling over each other to be heard.

'Nav, you take the wheel. I'm loading the cannons!'

'Oh shit, we've taken damage—I'm scooping out the water.'

'Bro, you're about to smash into a rock. Hard right! Hard right!'

Between the three of us, we managed to keep our little vessel afloat and soaring through the CGI waves, which at times tossed us with abandon while a fiery tornado pelted our deck with flaming stones, and at others bobbed us up and down before a brilliant sunset. We'd climb the mast to the top and take it all in. It's pretty incredible what gaming technology has achieved in just a generation. My childhood was spent watching a blocky Crash Bandicoot jump up and down on floating cubes of wumpa fruit. Now we lost ourselves careening through a world that made us forget briefly about the shuttered borders and hostile air outside our windows.

'Mo ... Mo!'

'What?'

'There's a ship. I see a ship. It's a big one!'

'Are we gonna go for it?'

'Hell yeah we are.'

I race back up to the helm and swing it all the way south. The bow begins to tilt starboard and the sails balloon and lurch us forward. At the bottom of the TV screen I see two cartoon pirates racing across the deck to the cannons. One is a tall, dark-skinned woman in a velvet coat and matching tricorn, lighting the fuses with her ruby-adorned hook. That's Nav. The other is a burly Levantine man with a ponytail and a large black beard. That's Mustafa. They both look like real pirates, scrambling to aim the cannons at a pitch-black galleon just above the horizon that was moving straight for us.

My controller vibrates wildly, and I hear the sound of cannon fire. I look up and realise they have already begun firing on us. The first three shots plop into the water nearby, but the fourth crashes into our side, sending a burst of light and smoke into the air.

'Shiiiit. Fire, fire!'

Two cannonballs lurch out of our humble schooner and miss them completely. I steal a quick glance at my phone and see my two mates scrunching their faces and taking aim. I turn back to the TV and swing the boat to the right, dancing around the enemy ship as it turns into us. Mustafa strikes their smallest mast and it cracks in half, sinking on its side like an inflatable tube man whose generator had been switched off.

'Yeah, the boys!'

As the two ships narrowly avoid a collision, I let go of the wheel and race to the side, whipping out my spyglass to get a look at the enemy team.

'Guys ... guys...'

'What?'

'...these aren't players.'

Through the fisheye lens I scan the ashen wooden deck of the ship, but instead of animated avatars jumping frantically to avoid our cannon fire, I see a crew of skeletons perched portside, their golden cutlasses raised in the air as they fire one decisive blow after another. At the helm, in a flaming amber doublet, is their pirate king. He twists his hollow skull slowly and stares directly at me, peering through the screen and into my soul, before he disappears below the waves, alongside his hoodooed crew and the entire galleon.

We had surely been spared a cursed death.

II

WHEN CAPTAIN JACK SPARROW FIRST GRACED our screens in 2003's *Pirates of the Caribbean: The Curse of the Black Pearl*, I was a highly impressionable fourteen-year-old boy, mesmerised by the open sea and dreaming of adventure. Gloriously unveiled, the weird pansexuality of Johnny Depp tore up the gospel of boy-band masculinity we had all narrowly survived in the '90s. This was no Blackbeard, dead-eyed, with cannon fuses tied behind his ears to scare his enemies, commanding an army of navy deserters to terrorise the West Indies. This wasn't even Captain Hook, cadaverous and untempered, haunting the dreams of children while scouting wearily for crocs. He was somewhere in between, a quick-witted buffoon, invariably drunk and darkly charming. Depp modelled his thick eyeliner and slurred speech on Keith Richards, but his sway resembled Jackie Chan in *Drunken Master*.

He was undeniably cool, at least to my teenage mind, and a breath of fresh air from the tired action-hero genre that sold the *Men's Health* alphabro archetype as what we were meant to aspire towards. Men were supposed to love cars and guns, and for me, nothing could be more dull.

Instead, I wanted to be a pirate. A few years later, I got my chance.

It was a fleeting and far-off chance, but it was real. I had signed up to a talent agency in Auckland expecting to make the big break into Hollywood my teenage self had prophesied. They sent me to get my first and only professional headshot, then to an auditions coach, who told me I'd be great as a builder or a personal trainer. I wasn't sure how to take that. It certainly wasn't the brooding anti-hero starring opposite ScarJo and stirring Oscar buzz that I'd been dreaming of. I turned down most of the roles I got emailed (furniture salesman, café attendant, Arab goat herder) because I was always working during audition times. I suddenly understood why most of the actors I knew worked casual jobs that didn't demand they offer unquestionable loyalty for a paycheque.

After a while it seemed my agent had given up on me. The emails trickled off. I did get one *Shortland Street* audition, as almost every New

Zealander has at some point in their life. I tried my best to twist my larynx and subdue my vowels to sound like a Kiwi, but it was no use. I was too foreign-sounding to be convincing on TV. My dreams began to deflate.

Then one day I got my big break. The email immediately piqued my interest: 'Are we able to see a self-tape from MOHAMMED HASSAN for the role of "Ghost Soldier" in *HERSCHEL?*'

Herschel wasn't the name of the movie, and for legal purposes I'm not supposed to tell you what movie it actually was. It was in fact the latest instalment of a franchise about pirates, to be filmed in Queensland, produced by Disney. I'll leave the rest to your imagination.

They asked me to send through a tape of me reading the lines laid out in the scene. It wasn't much, just four lines and then a lot of space where I'd pretend I was on the deck of a galleon staring out at crystal Caribbean waters. I could achieve that, right? I hadn't had any formal acting training, but I'd been waiting for this moment my whole life. There was just one catch: 'Accent: Mild Spanish or North African accent (if Egyptian is his natural accent, that is fine).'

What did that mean? I'd never seen a pirate with a North African accent before, let alone an Egyptian one.

It's not as if Muslim pirates didn't exist. The Barbary Corsairs ruled the Mediterranean Sea in the sixteenth century, raiding European coastal villages, seizing merchant vessels and selling their captured crew to the Ottomans as slaves and cheap labour. There were the infamous Turkish Barbarossa brothers, Oruç and Hızır Hayreddin, who fought to liberate Spanish colonies. The elder, Oruç, was dubbed 'Barbarossa' because of his thick red beard, and made a name for himself by helping to transport Muslim and Jewish refugees fleeing persecution in Spain after its reconquest by Catholic monarchs. He captured the island of Djerba in modern-day Tunisia, and later Algiers, stretching Ottoman dominion to the edge of the continent. He was made governor over the city, and ruled it for just two years before the Spanish sent ten thousand soldiers to recapture it and kill him, leaving his body on display at the city gates. Hayreddin, the younger sibling, then took on the Barbarossa name and continued to dominate the seas.

Perhaps the most fascinating of the Muslim pirates was Sayyida al Hurra, whose real name was Lalla Aicha bint Ali ibn Rashid al-Alami. Born to Andalusian nobles, her family was driven out of Granada during the Spanish conquest, and settled in the Moroccan city of Tétouan, where she married the governor and assumed rule when he died. Having never forgotten the humiliating defeat her people experienced in Spain, she made a pact with Hayreddin Barbarossa and turned to a life of piracy, assembling a fearsome fleet that fought to free captives from the Spanish and ruled the Western Mediterranean for decades, until she was overthrown by her son-in-law in 1542. The title she was forever known by, Sayyida al Hurra, translates as 'the Free Matriarch'. Pretty damn cool.

But none of these mighty figures ever made it to the Caribbean, and none of them had Egyptian accents. I didn't speak in an Egyptian accent the way my parents did, and I often cringed at how clumsily it collided the consonants. It replaced p's with b's, so 'party' became 'barty'. This would be forgivable, if Egyptians didn't also and inexplicably replace b's with p's, as in 'umprella' and 'chalkpoard'. Th's were transformed to z's; v's became f's. It wasn't glamorous, and made you sound like you had an aggressive case of the flu.

'Za *Birates of Za Carippean* was ferry good.'

Embarrassing. But that's what the producers wanted, so that's what had to be done.

I ran through the lines until they stuck, and practised different inflections as I'd learnt to do while memorising poems. Say it angry, say it softly, say it sadly. Find the right emotional tone.

Then I whipped out the accent, and everything immediately fell apart.

GHOST SOLDIER: 'Gabtin, zere is sumzing abbroaching on za horizon.'

Have you ever tried to 'do' your own accent? It's like trying to lick your elbow. Was I supposed to mimic my mother, the woman who taught me everything I know about the Quran and who wrote beautiful and captivating prose in Arabic only to be laughed at for her heavy bilingual tongue by people who'd never straddled two cultures?

I stumbled on my audition tape years later while clearing out an old laptop. It was an excruciating watch. I wore an ill-fitting black t-shirt and stood with my back to our garage door, while off screen, my sister Basma read out prompts.

THE CAPTAIN (Basma): Full to starboard! We'll sail to the edge and cross with the light!

GHOST SOLDIER (me): Aye, sir! All handz full and raise za main!

It was hard getting into character with only four lines to read, and little else in the way of prompts. It was harder trying to take my own voice seriously. It probably goes without saying that I never heard back from Disney.

It turns out I wasn't the only person of colour who auditioned for this role. Australian comedian Aamer Rahman, who alongside Nazeem Hussain is part of the duo Fear of a Brown Planet, was approached by his agent with the same brief.

'It didn't have any instructions apart from the script, so I just did a Cockney accent, the way most of the pirates and Jack Sparrow had,' he told me. 'I was trying so hard not to laugh when I was recording it. I didn't want my first time on screen to be me wearing a bandana and running around with a cutlass, speaking in a ridiculous accent.'

So he never sent in the audition tape. He told his agent he had lost it. Clearly Aamer had more pride than I did.

'It wasn't until much later, when I found out that you had also been offered it, with those instructions, that I realised the producers were definitely trying to cast some Brown people.'

British comedian Paul Chowdhry has a great bit from one of his shows about his own experience auditioning for the role. He was asked by the casting director to put on an Indian accent.

'I'm a sellout. My dad came to this country in 1964, fought racial oppression in the streets of England. I was born in the '70s, fought racists in the '80s and '90s, and now, currently...'

[Puts on a thick Indian accent] 'Pirate Barbarossa, looking for deckhands, bastard.'

When the aforementioned blockbuster was released, I watched it curiously, trying to figure out who the role had ultimately gone to.

For more than two hours, I watched Jack Sparrow and his affable crew sail around the world, fighting British aristocrats and undead Spanish galleons. But not a single Brown pirate in sight. Surely I'd missed something. Was I watching the right movie? I turned back to the beginning, trying to figure out where the scene I'd been sent had ended up.

Then, about half an hour into the film, I found it. As Javier Bardem's doomy ghost captain Salazar runs across the skeletal deck of an impressive CGI ship, somewhere off screen I hear something that sounds familiar.

'Gabtain ... What iz habbening?'

That was it—the four lonely lines reduced to a single one, the character edited out of the film save a voice likely recorded in post-production, but the accent was unmistakable. Somewhere out there, an Egyptian actor had snatched his big break, only to have his face erased in favour of more screen time for the Hollywood A-lister. Ain't showbiz a cruel mistress?

Still, what a wasted opportunity. That disembodied pirate voice could've been me.

17

A letter unsent

DISCLAIMER: For reasons pertaining to national security, some of the contents of this letter have been redacted.

Dear Mohamed

You probably don't remember me, but we met two years ago, perhaps fortuitously, in the baggage claim area at Auckland Airport.

My name is XXXXXXXXXX and I am a Senior New Zealand Customs Officer.

You'd just hopped off a plane from Istanbul by way of Dubai and Melbourne, a twenty-six-hour journey with a few hours spared in transit. You looked exhausted, but upbeat. I could understand why.

You were returning to visit your parents for four weeks after having spent a year abroad in Turkey. It was the first time you'd been away from New Zealand for that long. You'd also travelled to the West Bank and Israel several times for work, Spain and Greece on holiday.

I know all this because I'd been watching you or, more accurately, tracing your flights across the sky, trying to decipher your world. Where were you going? What were your motives? Had you made contact with anyone suspicious during your travels, for example, XXXX or XXXXXX?

In my line of work they teach us to question everything. Find patterns where others may overlook. My supervisor and mentor XXXXXXXX once told me the most dangerous people are always the most unassuming. To suspect the unsuspected. To think of myself as a kind of lighthouse keeper on the shores of civilisation.

When XXXXXXXXXX made his infamous speech in 2005 about the militant underbelly of the Muslim community, I was sitting in the crowd nodding my head.

When Prime Minister XXXXXXX warned of jihadi brides flocking from our shores to fight with XXXX, I kept a watchful eye for anyone in my terminal who could fit the bill.

The Minister of Customs says there's no racial profiling at airports, that it's impossible to determine a person's religion from their passport details, but that's not entirely true. There are clues. When you've done this job as long as I have, you develop an eye for detail. A place of birth. Facial features. A tendency to XXXXXX.

A name like yours, for example, is a dead giveaway.

As such, I would say that our meeting was less serendipi tous than it was devised. I waited for maybe half an hour outside passport control before you showed up. I knew what you looked like because I printed out your passport photo. I knew what you'd be wearing because I watched the CCTV footage from outside the XXXXXXXX.

I waited for you to pick up your bags before I walked over, grabbed hold of your arm, and whispered: hey buddy, let's take a shortcut.

I could see your shoulders slouching. A resignation behind your eyes. I felt like a hunter who had finally cornered his prey. A Tom to your Jerry, perhaps. I am good at what I do.

In my report to Customs later that evening, I wrote:

▓▓▓▓▓▓▓▓▓▓▓▓▓▓ under direction from SupCO RA2251. Advised to inquire about photo in front of Dome of the Rock, when asked HASSAN replied, "I m Muslim, so what?"

Please note when HASSAN entered search he was calm and co-operative. ▓▓▓▓▓▓▓▓ *
* ▓▓▓▓▓▓▓▓▓▓▓▓▓▓▓▓▓▓▓▓▓▓▓▓ Due the time taken, and specifically the triage of his lap-top and phones he was quite angry by the end of the search. He was short with his answers, and fed up with the process.

I advised SupCO RA2251 of this immediacy after releasing HASSAN.

But you know this, because I know you OIA'd the report from my department. That was fine. I have nothing to hide, though I do admit I was disappointed. I was under the impression we were having a wonderful time getting to know more about each other—or really, me getting to know you.

But over those XXXXXX, you became more and more agitated. Combative. It's always the same with you people.

A few months before you landed, I stopped a Somali woman and her children for nine hours. Her eldest son, ten years old, complained over and over that he needed to use the bathroom and eventually we had to escort him. The other two fell asleep on the XXXXX.

Last month I got into a shouting match with a Syrian man who'd been stopped XXXXXXXX two years. He'd just flown back from Brisbane and didn't understand why we were questioning him.

It's in these times I return to my training and remind myself what's really at stake. Don't let my emotions get the better of me.

But there are times when the doubt creeps in. When the borders between good and evil blur.

On 15 March last year I stood in the middle of the terminal staring at my phone. Someone tuned the arrivals screen to the news and we huddled under it in silence. The footage of Hagley Park cordoned at one end played on a loop. A man wearing a long robe stained with something dark walked forward in a daze. An elderly woman in a hijab hugged what looked like a daughter in shock.

Over and over I watched this, the floor of my wits descending. The darkness dragging its hooves out from under my feet.

I drove home in silence, afraid to turn on the radio. When I arrived I walked to my daughter's bedroom, held her tight and wept. It was the first time I'd cried in years.

They said the youngest victim was from a Somali family. He was my daughter's age. I could not imagine what would happen if someone took her away from me. I don't know what I would do.

When they arrested the guy who did it, I could not stop looking at his face. Every few hours I would open the page and look at him again.

The police said he had arrived in New Zealand a year earlier, around the same time as you. He could've even been on the same flight. I can't shake the feeling that I've seen his face before. That he could have walked right past me as I waited for you outside passport control and I paid no attention to him. Found nothing to suspect. Focused instead on the task at hand. Focused on you.

Last week I took my daughter to visit our local mosque. We took off our shoes and walked in our socks over the fragile carpet. Sat in the corner and watched as the imam called to prayer. As the small congregation washed their faces, arms then feet and stood shoulder to shoulder in three rows. Hands folded over their hearts and their foreheads bowed. The imam read a passage from the Quran and I didn't understand it, but I felt something in me relax.

Afterwards, a man who looked just like my father walked over and sat with us, showed us pictures of his family and narrated the story of this place. How the community had run fundraising nights at the RSA for two years before they had enough money to rent out an old mechanic shop and turn it slowly into a place of worship.

On our way home, my daughter asked me why they prayed differently to the way we did. I told her we were all on different roads leading to the same house. The same way trees come in all shapes but reach towards the same sun. She smiled at me and then out at the world.

'I love the sun,' she said.

'Me too, baby.'

And so I decided to write to you, though I still don't quite know what I want to say. Maybe it's to say that I share your pain. Maybe it's to say that I understand something now that I didn't before. I get it. I see you. Maybe I just hope you know that.

That I see you now. I do.
Yours sincerely
XXXXXXXXXX

18

Two funerals

WHEN MY DAD FIRST ARRIVED IN New Zealand in 1996, he stayed in the spare room belonging to an elderly Egyptian couple for three months. In that time, Nazly and Abdulghani became his adopted parents in this foreign country.

Aunt Nazly was a sprightly matriarch, darting in and out of rooms mid-conversation, waving her arms wildly and talking to anyone who entered her house like they were a long-lost family member.

Once, while hosting us and our visiting grandfather for dinner, she disappeared suddenly from view for half an hour and returned with a dusty album from another era, full of sepia memories tracing to the 1930s and '40s. She perched herself in the middle of the room and flipped vigorously to a page in the middle, before declaring she had found the distant relative that linked our two families together.

Her husband Gedo Abdulghani always sat quietly in his armchair, making small conversation in the rare moments of silence but largely content with letting his matriarch fill the room.

He had been a high-ranking general and fought in the Arab–Israeli war in 1967, but now he sat in his armchair and slaved over the daily crossword, or watched Egyptian soap operas beamed in to the gigantic satellite dish his son Alaa had installed in their backyard.

During Ramadan, everyone would squeeze into their living room to watch the latest seasonal TV show from back home. A few years later other families set up satellite dishes in their own homes. You could probably see them from space, these aerial beams shooting up from all around the North Shore, searching for a familiar connection. A late-night hit of nostalgia to sedate the pain of distance.

Their home was a sun around which the rest of us new migrants revolved. On most weekends, they'd hold big dinners with open doors. Whenever they heard a new family had arrived in the country, they would reach out to welcome them, ask them what they needed, feed them, and hook them up with others in the community who could help.

My father, a thirty-four-year-old electrical engineer who may as well have been an astronaut on a mission to Mars, seeking life and economic opportunity there, found in them a sense of home. A familiar quiet in the chaotic uncertainty of migration.

He became especially close to their son Alaa, who married a Samoan woman named Gladys whom everyone adored. His firstborn daughter—the first Samoan–Egyptian I had ever met, and possibly the first there ever was—was named Nazly, after his mother. They would have two more children, Tafa and Maryam, and all three of them became doctors.

I don't know if it was because there were no other Egyptians when they first arrived in the late 1980s, or because they consciously wanted to plant roots in this country, but the circumference of their family stretched and grew.

The eldest, Uncle Emad, married into a Pākehā family in the '80s, then after a divorce married a Singaporean woman. The next two sons also married Pākehā women; then it was Uncle Alaa and Auntie Gladys; and then Uncle Amr whose partner was Māori.

At family gatherings, the feathers falling from the wings of their children and aunties and mothers-in-law and sisters and adopted kin like my father and mother would pile up in the living room and the kitchen and backyard. Glistening white feathers would float out the window on the summer breeze, around the tītoki trees and up the streets until they reached Apia and London and Singapore and Cairo and Tauranga.

In the welcome warmth of an October afternoon in 2020, I drove to a small mosque near Auckland Airport, where the rest of my community had gathered, to pray over Aunty Nazly before she would be buried. At the Manukau Memorial Gardens, we took turns shovelling dirt, her five sons now in their fifties and sixties, sweating through their button-up shirts, overcome by uncharacteristic silence.

I watched as, one by one, feathers floated down from the air and began collecting at the foot of her grave. Dozens of children who had danced and darted around the bones of her home were now men and women with families and careers, their infants cradled in their arms as they laughed with cousins they hadn't seen in months if not years. Young Nazly, the granddaughter, talked about trying to raise her two children between hospital shifts and asked excitedly if we were coming over later for food with everyone else.

My dad stood on the periphery, overcome with emotion in a way I had never seen before. His words trapped in his throat. His hat lowered to hide his eyes. Aunty Nazly was the last parental figure left in his life, and between the rush of memories he must have felt a strange loneliness seeping in.

When the grave was filled, our local imam, Sheikh Rafat, gathered us closer and told us that what we perceive as a dark hole in the ground, the triumph of dirt, was in fact a portal into another world—one that Aunty Nazly was now traversing alone, with the sum of her short life on this earth, and the numerous acts of kindness and connection she had provided for nearly everyone who stood with us that day. I thought about what this community she had built had meant for me, the shelter it had offered, and I asked myself what I had offered in return.

On the drive from the cemetery, my brother tells me it's strange how desensitised we've become to burials. I tell him it's healthy to be comfortable with death and reflect on it often, the way Islam tells us to. But I know what he really means. Like me, he's remembering those four days in March last year, in Christchurch, when we buried fifty-one people from our community.

Like dozens of other Muslims, me and my brother flew down from Auckland to help. All of the childhood friends I'd met at gatherings like the ones at Aunty Nazly and Gedo Abdulghani's house were there. Day by day, they drove to the cemetery and donned fluorescent vests to usher the mourners around a surreal sight. Fifty-one holes dug six feet deep, aligned side by side in five rows. I imagine they needed an Excel spreadsheet just to figure out the logistics of who would go where. Whose body had been released by the coroner first, washed and wrapped in cotton and readied for the journey.

Over a makeshift speaker system, another childhood friend, Bilel, read out each name, and called the family to come forward. A group of six or seven lifted up the body and walked it a hundred metres through the crowd until it reached its home. The opening passage of the Quran was read out, and then we lined up, heaped a mound of dirt in our hands, and gently threw it in. Then my brother motioned people to make way, before Bilel read out another name and the ceremony began again.

From Tuesday until Friday, for five hours at a time, this is all we did. In the morning we would all stand with the bodies laid out in front of us and pray the funeral prayer. In the evening we would visit the families, Sheikh Rafat out front, telling stories about his memories of each of the departed, and describing in vivid colour the journey they were now on.

On Friday afternoon, as the final body was lowered into the ground, everyone on site broke down together. A week of leveed tears finally allowed to flood.

Maybe it's a sign of trauma to make connections between seemingly disconnected memories. The natural death of an elderly matriarch and the unnatural death of a congregation. But in times of distress our memories tend to collapse on top of each other. We look for patterns in the chaos to help us make sense. All of my conversations in New Zealand return inevitably to Christchurch. It is like a glitch in time. A rupture in the VHS film that keeps replaying a loop of a memory.

My brother tells me on the drive home from Manukau that he avoids attending Friday prayers now. That he can't bring himself to take his two young sons to the mosque. That he doesn't feel like he can protect them there.

In the aftermath of March 15, attacks against the Muslim community haven't stopped. Several groups, including the Islamic Women's Council, have been the subjects of targeted campaigns of abuse. A study from The University of Auckland found Islamophobic abuse rose by 1300 per cent. These findings are still based mostly on anecdotal data because the police have refused to implement a hate crime registry.

When I walk into a mosque on a Friday, a small part of my brain is imagining worst-case scenarios. A stranger with ill intentions entering through the door as our backs are turned, kneeled in prayer. A driver caught in a moment of rage who swerves on to the footpath as we're leaving to return to our lives. Or simply a hateful word hurled from a speeding car that will leave us on edge for the rest of the day. The presence of police outside the mosques is both welcome and jarring. The worshippers floating in and out like white feathers now look like they could blow away any minute.

After March I asked myself what this country meant to me, and what I mean to this country. The strange loneliness I had felt on my first day of school in 1997, the loneliness my dad felt at Aunty Nazly's funeral, returned. The sense of belonging I'd spent my entire life chasing now felt hollow. Everything had become a mirror.

•

I spent the better part of twenty-five years waiting for someone to hand me a certificate that tells me that I am the same as everyone else. That promises safety and warmth to my two little nephews, dancing around our feet in their uncomplicated joy. This is not the world I want them to inherit.

Unlike me, they will not grow up questioning whether they belong in this country, because this country will be the only home they know. But what does that belonging mean?

I am still figuring that out, but an image is beginning to form in my head. If belonging is a state of being, it is also a verb. An act of resistance. If I am to belong, then I must will it for myself. If my nephews are to belong, then it is on me to build for them the country that can hold them. The house through which they can dance and sing, their wings outstretched and soaring.

At the sentencing hearing in August 2020, a man who looks an awful lot like my father speaks from his soul. He says, 'My brothers and sisters suffered but we are stronger than ever before.' His name is Mirwais Waziri, and he is a national hero.

A woman who looks an awful lot like my sister speaks through anger and beauty and pain. She says, 'In the end, love will always win'; that the events of March 15 have 'woven us a thread that is far more integral in the fabric of New Zealand society than ever before'. Her name is Sara Qasem, and she is a national hero.

Ninety-one survivors, family members, fathers, daughters, best friends bared their wounds for the country, and the world, to see. One after another, they read searingly honest accounts of what they had lived through, both on that Friday in March 2019 and in every moment since. Each story deserved its own space, its own courtroom, its own country to mourn alongside.

Abdelfattah Qasem. Atta Alayan. Haji-Daoud Nabi. Linda Armstrong. Husna Ahmed. Ali Elmadani. The forty-five others whose names and faces deserve to be etched into the consciousness of our present moment, and our history books, forever. The survivors still struggling with surgeries, trauma and upended careers. The families who carried their grief in and out of police stations, media interviews and courts of justice to ensure a man who is a danger to all of us remains behind bars for good.

They don't deserve only our sympathy, but our gratitude. They have done the unimaginable, and now they must be allowed to continue their healing in peace, knowing that a team of five million is holding space for them always, in our hearts, in our history, in our story.

Two months later, I stand at the foot of Aunt Nazly's grave and look around in awe at the world she had created, the seeds she had sown, planted and nurtured for more than six decades, and I see a new New Zealand that has sprung forth into life. A soft-spoken one that willed itself into being. That needed no one's approval or acceptance.

Its wings unfurling under a perfect blue sky. Its gentle feathers falling all around us, shimmering in the infant-summer glow of a sun that climbs higher and higher, lifting its head from an early grave and floating up and up and up and into the heavens. A matriarch ascending. A guiding light that illuminates us all. This tiny community of ours shining with purpose, a commitment to grow, to resist, to belong.

And, dare I say it, to hope.

19

10 stages of Arabic love

AL HAWA—ATTRACTION

The iconic Egyptian singer Abdel Halim Hafiz sang of walking in a drunken state through the streets of Cairo, being whipped one way then another by the wind. In Arabic, *hawa* means both wind and lust, an unreliable force that lifts and twists unexpectedly. It comes as a gentle breeze or a hurricane, sending a chill down your spine or destroying your village.

You are way hotter than in the photos. Your laugh is like a match lit in a cave. The gravity of the room bends itself around you as you talk, eyes wild with intent, piercing through awkward silences. You tell me you love Sylvia Plath and Bukowski. What am I getting myself into?

Al Sabwa—Amusement

We have our first date in London, on neutral ground. It's also my birthday, so you buy me socks with caricatures of Picasso, Van Gogh and Pinto, and then pull out a card game from your bag.

'Have you ever played the confessions game? You pick a random card and then you have to answer the question written on it as honestly as you can.'

I draw the first card: *In what ways has your family damaged you?*

Outside the Korean BBQ spot waiting for an Uber, a homeless man stops to ask for change, then glances between us with a smirk.

'Is this thing romantic?'

We laugh nervously and avoid eye contact. He smacks his thighs with delight and disappears in a poof of smoke.

Al Shaghaf—The outer layer of the heart

Dating in the twenty-first century is like playing dice with macaques. Make the wrong move and the monkey makes off with the dice and your lunch. The spice of attraction was ruined by HBO and reality TV, and millennials learned the hard way the internet wasn't our friend. We stare at each other across the table, trying to predict the future, the gravity between us swelling and throbbing.

'I really wanna hold your hand right now.'
'Do you think that's a good idea?'
'No.'

Al Wajd—Preoccupation

At King's Cross we wrap ourselves into each other. You hold on for a second longer and whisper:

'You're a special one.'

I watch your silhouette fade into the gray of the train station and close my eyes. Somewhere lost in the expanse of me, a lumbered white dwarf explodes into a nebula. Neil deGrasse Tyson would have wept at the sight.

Al Kalaf—Infatuation

'So, I have something I want to say.'

I hold your hands in mine the moment we reach the lookout, a hidden terrace overlooking the glorious Bosphorus, frequented by students rapt in the whiff of love. It's the most romantic place I know of as a foreigner in a strange city, and so I chose it for this moment.

You look back with your eyebrows raised. My ankles melt into English mustard. The monkeys return to drum against my liver. The stars spin feverishly. I swallow and look into the daring browns of your eyes.

'Sam ... I love you.'

You grin. The stars slow to a gentle waltz. Our hands squeeze closer. Then a shadow steps into the light.

'Afedersiniz efendim...'

A young Turkish man with a hand outstretched, swaying with the stars. A bottle of Efes twirling over his shoulder. I put my hand up to say 'no thank you', but he insists.

'Lira alabilir miyim?'

Can I have a lira? Romance ruined.

Al Najwa—Heartburn

Najwa is a common woman's name in Egypt, though we turn the 'jah' into a 'gah' like we do with everything, robbing the Arabs of their eloquence. It derives from the word for 'salvation', describing a state of helplessness two lovers find themselves in.

You have a rule about never saying goodbye. The sentimental poet in me hates it. I want to savour every second, hold everyone I cherish inside my palms and press them to my cheeks. Every time I drop you off at the airport I feel the vines twisting around my arms. You walk away without looking back, and only when you sit on the plane do you take out your phone.

'I miss you.'

Al Shawq—Longing

I have written to the International Olympics Committee to lobby them into including long distance relationships at the 2024 Paris games. It's about time seasoned professionals like us got the recognition we deserve. Falling in love at long distance is an endurance sport, one that involves scheduling, patience, humour and above all; learning to live by yourself after you've found someone you can't stand to be away from.

Between Istanbul and Riyaad is simpler. You call me half-asleep in the morning. I send you voice notes at lunch time. We reconvene in bed as we mull sleep. New Zealand on the other hand is a nightmare. Nine hours of difference is an ocean. I wake up too late and miss you before you sleep. You start your shift just as I end mine. We can't wait until I'm back in the northern hemisphere so we can be lonely at manageable hours. It's March 2020, and we don't know everything's about to change.

Al Wasab—Excruciating pain

The Arabic poets reveled in heartache. They wrote long odes to the desert sands, the migrating birds and the melancholic steeds. All were metaphors for a lover waiting in a distant village, or the memory of an unrequited childhood crush that ended up with a richer man. Romance was heightened through extreme periods of longing, and true love was a destined reunion years in the making. Yes, we're an intense bunch.

When the pandemic hits, our experiment in professional longing becomes a permanent reality. I'm suddenly trapped under lockdown in Auckland, and you make it to your parent's house in Khobar just in time before a nationwide curfew sets in. The days stretch into months, then years. We try to catch each other through time zones.

'Hey, are you up?'
'Sorry in a meeting.'
'Why didn't you call?'
'Can you video?'
'Where are you?'

Al Kholla—Unification

A year and a half later, I hustle an early second dose of the vaccine so I can fly into Cannes to see you. It's the first time you've been allowed out of the country. We lower our masks and stare at each other over ravioli di zucca, which you apologise isn't as good as you remember.

'Hi.'

'Hey.'

When you finish work, we climb to the top of La Croix Des Gardes and watch the French celebrate their empire by setting the sky on fire. You wrap your arm around mine and we let the anguish of distance melt into the sea.

Al Gharam—Fervour

I stand outside the room trying to stuff the shirt into my pants so it would sit flat. I've been told to wait, and the nerves have begun sinking in. I look around and try to remember this moment. Kate re-emerges and calls me in. And there, in a fountain of pink and white, is you. A green and white bouquet bursting from your hands. Silk tulle falling over your eyes, piercing and fiery as they always are. I stop, unable to piece together words. What would Abdel Halim say at this moment? What would Bukowski?

'Wow.'

It's all that's left on my tongue, and nothing more can suffice. Your mother clasps a hand to her heart. The makeup lady bursts into tears. I step forward, and lift the veil over your face. Time stops in its tracks. The monkeys hold their breath. My lungs gibber and whoop and I try to stay composed. I have reached the surface of the sun, and she smiles at me like I am someone special. Someone worth loving. We hold hands and walk into the light. The planets dance around us, singing the songs our grandmothers used to sing. For a single moment, we are here together. It is all we have wanted for an age and maybe more. For a single moment now, all in the universe is good.

Acknowledgements

MY UNENDING GRATITUDE TO EVERYONE WHO helped me on this journey, whose love, support and friendships sustained and watered me: my beautiful parents, Basma, Sherif and Reem and Zayn and Zak, Teta, khalto Aliyah, khalto Neveen, my dear Samaher, Ken Arkind, Carrie Rudzinski, Grace Taylor, Dominic Hoey, Nav, Mustafa, Canan, Asmaa, Aamer, JJ, Hassan, Omar, Faisal, Haroun, Ahmed Osman, Ahmed Youssef, Claire Murdoch, Anna Hodge, Paula Green, Rachael King, the Youssef Family, the Wax Boys, Sheikh Raafat, Ivanka, my Muslim community overflowing with grace and promise, Yasmine and Tom Ryan, Allah.

'A stranger in no man's land' was first published in *Newsroom* in July 2020.

'Still life with a pool of dreams' was first published in *The Pantograph Punch* in May 2020.

'A letter unsent' was performed as part of Verb Wellington at the National Library in November 2020.

'Two funerals' was performed as part of WORD Christchurch Festival in November 2020.

About the author

MOHAMED HASSAN is an award-winning poet, journalist, podcaster and producer from Auckland and Cairo.

He is the author of the anthology *National Anthem* (Dead Bird Books, 2020), which was shortlisted for the Ockham NZ Book Awards in 2020, and was the 2015 NZ National Slam Champion.

His poems have been shared widely online, and are taught in hundreds of schools internationally. He has toured his work across New Zealand, Australia, the US and UK, at TEDx and at the Cheltenham Literature Festival, and he represented NZ at the Individual World Poetry Slam in 2016.

Hassan was nominated for an Online Media Award in 2018 for his work covering the Israel/Palestine conflict, and his RNZ podcast Public Enemy was awarded the Gold Trophy at the 2017 New York Festivals Radio Awards.

'Mohamed Hassan takes the things we universally love—food, music, family, dreams of travel, a heart's desire—and affirms their gorgeous ordinariness. Then he reveals how othering shatters what we share; how it splinters "us" to create confusion, ignorance, hurt and even hate. Sometimes his writing is gently observational, sometimes sad, sometimes justly angry, but always important, timely and true.'

—JOHN CAMPBELL

'The book is amazing. Mohamed Hassan is so talented. In *How To Be A Bad Muslim*, he pulls off that rare trick of taking a poet's grace and applying it to his essays, making them as beautiful to read as they are illuminating.'

—DOMINIC HOEY

'Mohamed's is a fresh voice but most of all, an important voice. We already have his poetry, which has been rightly recognised, but now New Zealand literature is all the richer for his elegant and powerful non-fiction.'

—RACHAEL KING

'Mohamed Hassan writes from a space that nobody else stands in; a space borne of deep understanding and lived experience. He is Muslim, a child of Egypt and the Middle East and a child of New Zealand; a global traveler and reporter with his finger very firmly on the socio-politics of the globe and our place in it. He has a depth of vision, a level of craft and a talent not seen elsewhere. His is a voice that is vital. We need this book, now more than ever.'

—TUSIATA AVIA

'These essays navigate migration and grief, Islamaphobia and love, family and society. Kaleidoscopic in tone, they sear at both the personal and the political level, and open up the immigrant experience. There is no other book like this published in Aotearoa. It refreshes our views of the world and of each other.'

—PAULA GREEN

Back Cover Material

Award-winning New Zealand writer Mohamed Hassan blends storytelling, memoir and non-fiction to map the experience of being Muslim in the twenty-first century.

From Cairo to Takapuna, Athens to Istanbul, Hassan speaks authentically and piercingly on identity, Islamaphobia, surveillance, grief and loss.

He weaves memories of being an Egyptian immigrant fighting childhood bullies, listening to life-saving '90s grunge and auditioning for vaguely-ethnic roles in a certain pirate movie franchise. Funny, elegiac and lyrical.

'[Hassan] pulls off that rare trick of taking a poet's grace and applying it to his essays, making them as beautiful to read as they are illuminating.'
DOMINIC HOEY

'New Zealand literature is all the richer for his elegant and powerful non-fiction.'
RACHAEL KING

'Mohamed Hassan writes from a space that nobody else stands in ... His is a voice that is vital. We need this book, now more than ever.'
TUSIATA AVIA

'Kaleidoscopic in tone, these essays sear at both the personal and the political level, and open up the immigrant experience.'
PAULA GREEN